*The Working Parents'
Guide to Child Care*

The Working Parents' Guide to Child Care

Bryna Siegel-Gorelick, Ph.D.

LITTLE, BROWN AND COMPANY   **BOSTON • TORONTO**

The author is grateful for the material reprinted by permission of the New York University Press from *Behavioral Individuality in Early Childhood* by Alexander Thomas et al. Copyright © 1963 by New York University.

LIBRARY OF CONGRESS CATALOGING IN PUBLICATION DATA

Siegel-Gorelick, Bryna.
    The working parents' guide to child care.

    Bibliography: p. 209
    Includes index.
    1. Children of working parents.   2. Married
people—Employment.   3. Day care centers.   4. Baby
sitters.   5. Foster home care.   6. Education,
Pre-school.   I. Title.
HQ777.6.S55   1983   362.7'12   82-17121
ISBN 0-316-79004-4
ISBN 0-316-79003-6 (pbk.)

BP

Designed by Janis Capone

Published simultaneously in Canada
by Little, Brown & Company (Canada) Limited

PRINTED IN THE UNITED STATES OF AMERICA

*To
Steven
and
Alyssa*

Acknowledgments

Many people provided me with the resources needed to complete this book. Most of all, I received continued support before, during, and since this project from my husband, Steven Gorelick. Over the years, he has helped me see that I have the ability to make accomplishments that I feel are important. This has been the keystone of my personal and professional development. I thank him for his persisting belief in my strengths.

My source of spiritual support has been my daughter, Alyssa. Through her, I understand parenting and child development in a way that no psychologist can learn in a classroom or laboratory.

Support from friends has enabled my work, too: Rosanne Kermoian has stimulated me with ongoing discussions of this material; Ted Clay and Colleen Horner have contributed by helping me relax after days of writing, when, by evening, I was overstimulated, exhausted, or both.

The research environment at the Stanford University Division of Child Psychiatry and Child Development, where I work, has been a source of vitality and new ideas. I am particularly grateful to Professor Thomas Anders, Head of the Division, for his constant support.

Yet another valuable source of input has been years of formal and informal dialogues with parents and caregivers of children in day care. There is no way to thank all these people as individuals. I hope in reading this book some of you will recognize your situations, and feel that your problems and solutions have been presented in ways that will be instructive to newer parents.

B.S.G.
STANFORD, CALIFORNIA

Contents

The Working Parents'
Guide to Child Care

Introduction

WHAT'S THIS BOOK ABOUT? It's a book for parents who are considering various possible day care arrangements for their child. It explains what has been learned from years of careful, empirical research on day care, as well as from the experiences of many, many parents who have used day care. It draws upon hundreds of hours of systematic observation and comparison of children in different types of day care and at home. It is based on formal interviews and informal conversations with scores of parents who have used day care, and with numerous women who have provided day care in all kinds of settings.

As a child psychologist, I have done many years of field and experimental research on the effects of day care. However, I am also a parent, and a user of day care.

The purpose of writing this book was to help parents choose the best possible day care arrangement by bringing together information about the effects of day care, and about normal child development. To this end, the book highlights major research efforts on day care and child development. (The chapter reference section at the end of the book lists these studies, by chapter, for the interested parent or student of child development.) In addition to describing research on day care and development, this book will provide you with guidelines for developing skills for interviewing and observing in different day care settings, and practical information that you, as a user of day care, will need: lists of referral agencies, an explanation of the child care tax credit, sample day care contracts, and so on.

This book is for a variety of readers: expectant parents trying to decide how they feel about day care; for parents choosing day care for the first time; for parents deciding whether to change day care arrangements. Also, child care professionals will develop a better understanding of parental concerns about day care from this book. It will be equally useful to you whether you plan to have your child cared for in your own home, or whether you will use out-of-home day care.

The book will discuss, step by step, what types of day care there are, what your child's individual developmental needs will be in a day care arrangement, what services you can expect a day care arrangement to offer, how much you will pay, how to recognize good day care, how to help your child adjust to day care, and how to deal with any difficulties that arise.

Rather than giving just a brief outline of day care health and safety requirements, which general parenting books often present, this book will teach parents what is important to consider when looking for day care and why these things are important. This book is for parents who want to use the best available information to make their own educated decisions about their child's development, rather than blindly taking advice given by professionals.

The women's movement has brought into focus many problems associated with modern child-rearing: how much better it would be if working parents only had more flex-time, more job-sharing, extended maternity leave, and of course, better day care. However, this is not a feminist treatise. Often, feminist rhetoric offers no concrete or viable solutions to these already very obvious problems. This book offers one type of solution by helping you be a more discriminating consumer of day care. Then, we can hope to raise the standards for day care services that parents will expect and accept. When I talk about parents I am referring to mothers *and* fathers. Child care is a family issue, not "just" a women's issue. Fathers are participants in child care and deserve consideration, recognition, and the information they need to do the child-rearing they want to do, and to do it well.

My approach is to make you aware of wide-ranging aspects of your child's development that may be affected by being in day care. In doing this I have tended to be overcautious rather than undercautious, choosing to point out considerations that might not apply to all children

I make no unproven, untested statements concerning the length of time a mother "must" stay home following the birth of a child. I, and other child development professionals, simply don't know that. Instead, I outline the possible risks and benefits of day care at each age. I put emphasis on each child as an individual, with an individual set of risks and benefits that must be evaluated by parents, the people who know their own child best.

WHO USES DAY CARE?

Perhaps more families than you think use day care. Statistics abound on the numbers and ages of children in day care, and what kinds of day care are used. Different sources (such as various studies commissioned by the U.S. Bureau of Labor Statistics) give different estimates and different projections of day care use, but convey the same image.

Today, half of all American mothers work outside their homes. In 1978, 40 percent of children under six years old had working mothers. Out of the 11 million children in some form of day care in 1978, 2.5 million were infants and toddlers, 3.7 million were preschoolers, and 4.9 million were school-age children receiving after-school care.

Projections for 1982 indicate there will be 2.9 million infants, 4.3 million toddlers, and 5.8 million school-age children: a total of 13 million children in some kind of day care. Among children in day care for more than two hours a week, about 35 percent are believed to be cared for in their own homes (there are probably more than that); about 47 percent in another person's home (family day care); and about 18 percent in day care centers.

What will day care use in 1985 be? In 1990? In 1985, there are expected to be 6 million children under six years of age in day care. This will be an increase of about one-third over the preceding ten years. By 1990, 75 percent of all American mothers will be in the work force. Forty-five percent of all mothers of children under six years old are expected to be working. These women will have approximately 10.5 million children.

Day care is rapidly becoming the norm for families with children below school age. Until recently, children remained within the shelter of their families during these formative years. For many children, day care is their first experience outside their families. Parents are relinquishing direct control over their children's development as the children enter day care. Understanding day care gives parents a means, albeit a less direct means, of retaining control over their children's developmental course.

Chapter 1

What Types of Child Care Arrangements Are Available?

THE FIRST STEP in finding a good day care arrangement is to learn what types of care are available. There are three types of care: in-home care, family day care, and day care centers. In-home care refers to day care arrangements that take place in your own home. Family day care is an arrangement in which you take your child to someone else's home. In day care centers, several adults care for a group of children.

The purpose of this chapter is to acquaint you with these different types of day care. By the end of the chapter, you should have a good idea about which type of day care you will use.

The information is arranged by topic — for example, caregivers, programs, physical environment, peers — rather than by type of care so that you can compare each of the issues for each type of care. For purposes of comparison, in-home care and family day care are sometimes jointly referred to as home-based care because they both take place in a home, rather than in an institutional setting, such as a day care center. Other times, comparisons are made between in-home individual care and group care (meaning family day care and center day care).

Even if you have already decided on the type of day care that you want to use, read this chapter anyway, to broaden your perspective and perhaps discover new ideas that may change your mind about what type of day care is really most suitable. After you have read about what parents have found to be the best and the worst aspects of each of these types of care, you can decide for yourself what type of care you feel will be most beneficial for your child and for you.

CAREGIVERS

The word *caregiver* refers to adults who take care of children and is preferable to *caretaker, babysitter, childminder, day care provider,* and sometimes even *teacher,* for several reasons. The term *caretaker* is inaccurate since the adult is giving care, rather than taking it. *Caregiver* is the accepted term in scientific research on day care. It is a broad, generic term including all kinds of people who give care: mothers, fathers, relatives, friends, neighbors, babysitters, family day care mothers, and teachers. Caregivers will be referred to as she/her since women overwhelmingly comprise caregivers in all kinds of day care.

Another, different reason for using *caregiver* is that it is important for you, as a consumer of day care, to think of the person who is in charge of your child as a giver of care, a provider of a valuable service, and someone who is carrying out an important, professional role.

Some alternative terms for *caregiver* minimize the responsibilities of the job, for example, the word *babysitter*. You do not want a caregiver who merely "sits" there. You do not want your child treated like a baby if he is older and more developed than that. *Babysitter* is most typically associated with teenage girls who come over in the evenings when parents go out. In fact, they do a lot of "sitting," while the "baby" sleeps. A daytime caregiver needs to do so much more than that for your child. It is a little insulting to refer to a good caregiver who does her job well as *just* a babysitter. In fact, one article about what goes into making high-quality family day care (written by a day care mother) is titled "I'm Not Just a Babysitter!"

In day care centers, the caregiver is frequently called a teacher. This title may be justified when preschoolers are involved, but as far as infants and toddlers go, such "teachers" are no more likely to teach (in the formal sense of the word) than are various home-based caregivers. The title of *teacher* may provide parents of very young children with the illusion that there is some special instructional quality inherent in center day care that family day care or in-home care necessarily lacks. In fact, caregivers of very young children do essentially the same things, regardless of the type of care setting.

What to Look for in a Caregiver

Most child care experts are convinced that the caregiver is the single most important ingredient in a day care arrangement. She is your child's surrogate mother while you are away. Ideally, the caregiver should treat your child with the same care and love that you do when you are with your child. Different caregivers will react in various ways to your child as a result of their age, experience, family relationship to you, status as a child care professional, and individual personalities.

When you choose an in-home or family day care arrangement, you are, by and large, choosing a single caregiver. When you choose center day care, you'll have to weigh the characteristics of each caregiver who'll be with your child, as well as how those caregivers function as a team. Here are some general guidelines for helping you decide what to look for in a caregiver.

Age A caregiver's energy level and strictness or permissiveness are often related to her age. When using in-home care or family day care, you'll have to decide what age of caregiver is likely to best suit your child. You can expect that, generally, younger caregivers will have more pep than older ones. Older caregivers may have more experience and perhaps patience. Young caregivers are closer to their own childhoods, and may be more likely to remember what kids think is fun. They will get down on the floor and do silly things that make a six-month-old giggle. They (more than anyone else) have the energy to keep up with the endless physical gyrations of a small child, especially an unusually active child.

Older women may be excellent caregivers and truly enjoy looking after a little one. Such women may be considered unemployable in the general work force, and therefore may be more eager, lasting workers. An older caregiver, however, must be healthy and energetic enough to keep up with your child's demands. Many are: one fifty-year-old family day care mother I knew was in the habit of swimming a half mile, even in fifty-degree weather, every morning before the kids arrived. You wouldn't want your child sitting around watching soap operas every afternoon because your caregiver had no energy for anything else. Some day care mothers have teenagers living at home who help out and give the children more opportunity for roughhousing. Much older caregivers may be best suited for more sedentary tasks. A grandmother may be nicest for a very young infant. They can sit, rock, feed, burp, catnap, rock, feed, burp, and catnap. Older women may be less bored (and therefore more satisfied) with their work when it is largely limited to the housebound existence of a new baby in the wintertime. An older caregiver may be better able to handle your child if he is a "terrible two" and you fear he will be a "terrible three." Frequently, older caregivers are firmer disciplinarians than younger caregivers, who tend to be more permissive. (I do not mean to create ageist stereotypes here, but rather to state generalizations that have come from my observations and those of my colleagues.)

When using center day care, you can keep your eyes open for an age-mixed staff. Day care centers with what are referred to as multigenerational staffs are nice because they expose children to the perspectives that caregivers of different ages can bring. For children who live far from their grandparents, exposure to older adults in a caregiving role can be especially enriching.

Gender   For better or for worse, most caregivers are women. This phenomenon is of course related to the only recently easing social pressure on mothers to stay home with children who are below school age. When a child receives in-home care from someone who is not a woman, it is most often the child's father. (There's a special discussion of fathers as caregivers beginning on page 19.)

I have yet to meet (or hear about) a family day care father who runs his own show, although many husbands of family day care mothers do actively participate in taking care of the children. This is especially likely to be the case if the day care mother is an older woman and her husband is retired.

Day care centers are becoming more aware of the need to include men on their staffs. A larger proportion of single mothers compared to two-parent families use centers. Male caregivers at the center may be the closest that children of single mothers come to experiencing a male in a nurturant role. This is important because outside the privacy of the home, men are seldom seen in caring roles with children.

Unless you are a single mother and your child doesn't have an ongoing relationship with any adult man, don't be overly concerned with finding an arrangement with a male caregiver. Think of a day care arrangement that includes both men and women caregivers as one with an extra plus.

Language A good caregiver will speak frequently and directly to your child in a clear fashion that is appropriate for your child's level of comprehension, something that good caregivers do intuitively. Psycholinguists have dubbed the simplified, high-pitched, repetitive, monosyllabic way of talking to children as *motherese*. It has been shown repeatedly to be a key factor in the fostering of language development.

In some areas of the country, caregivers tend to come from ethnic minorities. This is especially true of in-home caregivers and family day care mothers. These women lack training and work permits that would enable them to be employed outside their homes. In addition, there is frequently a language barrier involved.

There are a number of pros and cons to having a caregiver who speaks a language other than English as her first language. First, a lot depends on how well she speaks English and which other languages you speak. If the only language that you have in common is English, then she should speak it well enough to communicate effectively with you.

More important, she should speak English grammatically. Little children learn language at an incredible rate. They are learning to speak even before they actually say anything. One of the reasons that children can acquire language so rapidly has to do with a process whereby they are continually formulating and modifying rules of pronunciation, semantics, and syntax. Children develop these rules on the basis of limited observations and modify them when they become aware of enough exceptions to them. For example, children will tend to use the word *is* before they use the word *are*. They say *he is, she is, they is, we is*. After a while, children realize that *are* means the same thing as *is* but is used when more than one person or object is being referred to.

Much of the day, your child will be influenced by the caregiver's way of speaking. If she is consistently ungrammatical, you can expect your child to pick up such inaccuracies. This is especially true for one- and two-year-olds, who are in the most formative period of language acquisition.

If your child is exposed to only occasional doses of a foreign language (say, between a day care mother and her husband), it certainly won't confuse your child's language development. In fact, it may help your child establish the concept of language — that there are other sets of words besides English. (My daughter has heard both Hindi and Farsi in her day care arrangements. From time to time she speaks gibberish and claims that it is one of these languages.) Another thing I wouldn't worry about is a caregiver's accent, if the structure of her language is well formed.

In some circumstances, having a caregiver who speaks another language may be an advantage. For example, a Chicano family I studied was comprised of a father who was a lawyer and a mother who worked as his legal secretary. They had both come from Spanish-speaking homes but no longer used Spanish together, although their families still did. They found a day care mother who spoke only Spanish to their one- and four-year-old girls. This way, the children heard and learned some Spanish, and could communicate with their Spanish-speaking relatives, although English was their predominant language when they were away from day care.

Unless you are bilingual in the same language as your child's caregiver, I would discourage the use of one language in day care and another at home. Children really don't seem to learn a language that is not reinforced by their parents and is not spoken in the culture in which they live. (Some, maybe all, of my colleagues in bilingual education might disagree with this view.) Since the second language wouldn't be spoken in the child's own home, and exposure to it would cease with the inevitable end to the particular day care arrangement, such efforts are often superfluous in the long term.

Training and Experience   How does the amount of formal training a caregiver has had relate to how well she cares for children? Is her practical experience in raising her own children important to consider? It is typical to find that in-home caregivers and family day care mothers have had no formal training dealing with children but have probably raised children of their own. Nearly the opposite is true for day care centers: caregivers tend to have at least a junior-college-level Child Development Associate (CDA) credential, an Early Childhood Education credential, or, in some places around the country, a Bachelor of Arts degree. Such women, however, usually do not yet have children of their own, so their training may exceed their experience.

Two studies, one in Pasadena, California, and another in St. Paul, Minnesota, looked at changes in family day care mothers after they'd received some training or had become part of a formal network of day care services. Sponsorship of network members typically included child development classes, group discussions, toy loans, planned field trips for the children, and time at a developmental nursery school. These studies have shown that formal training is likely to make a good caregiver better, but is not likely to make a bad caregiver good. It is not likely to make someone who is uninterested in children become interested in them.

When you *do* evaluate a caregiver's training, you should consider just what it is that she has been trained to do. The focus of the caregiver's training is very relevant. Please do not select a nurse (i.e., R.N. or L.P.N.) to care for your child on the basis of her medical training alone. Childhood is not a disease or disability! Probably the worst day care that ever existed was the World War II war nurseries (for example, in England) where well-intentioned child care focused on keeping children sanitary and out of germ contact with one another. Lack of sufficient human contact left many children retarded, while in extreme cases, infants died from what was termed marasmus or hospitalism. Surrounded by doctors and nurses, these babies literally died of loneliness.

Some day care centers hire former elementary-school teachers, but their training is not necessarily appropriate to caregiving. Experience with fourth-graders is largely not transferable to working with eighteen-month-olds. Experience with older children might be the source of inappropriate expectations and demands on the part of a caregiver who is unaccustomed to a roomful of babies. On more than one occasion I've witnessed a caregiver demanding that a crying twenty-month-old "Stop acting like a baby!" On the other hand, a schoolteacher is often someone who really likes children and adapts well to the demands of a new age group.

Researchers from the National Day Care Study observed children and caregivers in fifty-three day care centers in Detroit, Atlanta, and Seattle. They concluded that the level of formal education per se did not really matter. Instead, they found that a caregiver's specialized training was more closely related to how well she interacted with children. The most useful caregiver training was in pertinent fields, such as child development or early childhood education. This sort of training usually focuses on programs and activities for preschool-age children. Since day care for infants and toddlers is relatively new, compared to preschool education, there are few established programs that specialize in teaching caregivers how best to deal with children under three years old.

When it comes to dealing with very young children, some people have it and some just don't. Fortunately, those who don't usually steer away from child care careers. From what I've seen, caregivers with an innate ability to understand children gain as much from practical work experience as they do from training. Someone who loves children and has raised some of her own will be quite likely to stimulate the growth of your child in all the right ways. In some ways, classroom training may be thought of as a substitute for "hands-on" experience with children. Therefore, it is especially important that caregivers who are not parents themselves have training or other day-to-day experiences with children.

Professional Identity Another factor that bears on how well a caregiver does her job has to do with her ability to grow as a child care professional and to take satisfaction from the job she is doing.

This is probably most difficult for in-home caregivers, who are least likely to be in contact with other caregivers.

Similarly, family day care mothers sometimes feel isolated and unrewarded. Some family day care mothers know other family day care mothers or belong to associations or networks. Through these contacts, they can share experiences and get ideas for new activities from one another. However, such contact tends to be informal and infrequent. (If you cared for five kids from 8:00 A.M. until 6:00 P.M., would you want to go to a meeting at 7:30 P.M. to talk about day care until 9:30 P.M.?)

Caregivers in day care centers definitely have the edge when it comes to professional contact and exchange of ideas. They talk with their co-workers each day, and constantly observe and learn from one another in action. In addition, good centers have regular staff meetings where directors and others introduce ideas for new activities and ways of dealing with problems.

Caregivers decide what your child will and will not do. This is very important because young children learn through doing. Caregivers can make all the difference in the world in determining whether your child enjoys and learns during day care hours. When you have your child cared for in your own home, your choice of caregiver is all the more crucial. The caregiver is the largest single source of social, emotional, and cognitive stimulation, all of which are essential for positive development.

In-Home Caregivers

In addition to general good qualities to look for in any caregiver, there are some additional things to consider when choosing a caregiver who will work in your home. There are several types of in-home caregivers, each with advantages and disadvantages, depending upon your personal situation, including:

- a family member
    your sister, sister-in-law, cousin, or other female relative
        about your own age
    an older relative (your child's grandmother, grandaunt,
        or other older person)
    the child's father

- a paid caregiver
  a housekeeper doing child care and housework
      live out
      live in
  a child care worker doing only child care
      live out
      live in (an au pair, nanny, or governess).

Family Members   In days gone by, many people lived in extended families; that is, in a household shared with relatives. In those days, grandmothers, aunts, and older siblings could take care of younger children if a mother worked. Extended families are becoming extinct in these days of great geographic mobility. Most of us no longer have the alternative of day care provided by another adult family member who lives with us. Some of us, though, do live with relatives or have them nearby. Still others may want to consider having a relative move in, expressly for the purpose of providing child care. Anyone who lives in your home will know quite a bit about your child before you ever leave your child with her. Also, an extended-family member will be someone with whom your child is familiar. Third, a relative who lives with you will have had an opportunity to gain a good understanding of your ideas about raising children. Of course, these qualifications of being known by and knowing the potential caregiver may be true of any relative or friend who visits or is visited regularly.

You may not think of your relative caring for your child in your house as day care, but that is exactly what it is. If you work, and choose to have a family member care for your child, that person has to be just as dependable and just as professional about her work role as any other caregiver.

There are many reasons why parents often consider having their child cared for by a relative to be the best possible arrangement. The younger a child is, the more likely the parents are to choose in-home care. The decision to find an in-home care arrangement is often based on the great need infants have for almost constant, individual care. Having your child cared for by relatives may be a wonderful solution to your need for child care. A relative is someone who, almost by definition, loves your child and wants her to develop into the best possible adult. We expect relatives to be interested in the long-term development of the child. If you ask any grandmother what she wants her grandchild to be, she might say "a doctor," or "a lawyer," or "whatever will make her happy." If you posed the same question to a caregiver in a day care center, she probably wouldn't have a ready answer. You really wouldn't expect her to. We imagine that a grandmother will spend more hours stimulating a child's curiosity because of her expectations for that child. Certainly, we expect the grandmother to be more loving, physically expressive, and emotional about her relationship to her charge.

Before selecting a relative to care for your child, think about what kind of relationship you and she have. For better or for worse, the way your relative feels about you will probably be reflected in how she interacts with your child. Consider the philosophy of child-rearing that your relative would use when caring for your child. Will it reflect your way of doing things? What exactly does philosophy of child-rearing mean? If you and your mother-in-law disagree on schedules of feeding, amounts of TV watching, age for toilet-training, and methods of discipline, you have different philosophies of child-rearing. Do not use her as a caregiver. You will be asking for trouble. If you're not sure of her philosophy, watch her in action. It is more important to see what she does, rather than hear what she says she does. If you notice that she frequently picks up the baby after you've put her to bed, feeds the baby when you are sure she isn't hungry, and urges you to use cloth diapers rather than disposables, do not use her as a caregiver. But if you feel the same way about these things, you can expect a day care arrangement between you to work out well.

If you have never discussed specific child-rearing practices with your prospective relative/caregiver, do so before starting an arrangement. What is most important is an understanding and a willingness for the caregiver to yield to the parents' wishes on important matters; this is something any parent has the right to expect. Follow-through on parents' child-rearing philosophy is as necessary an ingredient for a good day care arrangement as love for the child and eagerness and willingness to do well.

Beware of the "grandmother-knows-best" syndrome. The relationship between you and your own parent or parent-in-law may get in the way of using your child's grandmother as a caregiver. If she still thinks of you or your spouse as her child, there may be deep-seated psychological blocks that will prevent her from readily carrying out your wishes.

Realize, however, that no one, probably not even your spouse, will treat your child exactly in the style that you would. Some variety in personal styles is desirable. It will help your child learn that people are different and will react differently toward her. What you want to avoid is having your child receive mixed messages. Uncertainty about limits to behavior makes children anxious.

Grandmothers, who are frequently older, retired, or nonworking women, as well as experienced in child-rearing, are the most likely caregiver candidates for many families. But what about a member of your own generation, such as a sister, sister-in-law, or cousin? If you do select a relative your own age, she should have had experience with her own children or experience with children in some sort of work setting. Consider that the "balance of power" may be upset by your becoming her boss, which you will be in some sense, since you will be making the major decisions about your child's well-being while under her care. You will have to consider and decide whether your temperament and her temperament will withstand the give and take necessary for a successful day care arrangement.

Another version of in-home day care by family members is care provided by a child's older sibling. This form of day care has been much decried. Shocking statistics abound on the numbers of "latchkey" kids, children at home without adult supervision. There is reason to be shocked and saddened by the fact that so many parents behave so irresponsibly. Certainly children under seven or eight years old should never be left alone with each other for any extended length of time. No matter how grown up or responsible children may act, they simply have not had enough time to develop the capabilities for making complicated decisions in unusual circumstances.

Some of what has been written about "latchkey" children definitely has been overblown. Having a third-grader boy come home after school with his fourth-grader sister, watch TV, do homework, and set the table for dinner is not a horrible scenario. Of course, it is preferable for such children to be supervised, for example, by a neighbor or block parent who lives close by.

Anthropological studies of child-rearing of Third World countries revealed that the average age for caregivers of very young children was eight years old. Eight-year-olds certainly have the endless energy that is required for entertaining preschoolers. However, even in these countries, extended-family adults are around to take care of emergencies.

Some of you may have a teenage daughter, or sister who lives with you. This is becoming more common with the high rate of divorce and remarriage. Many couples have children and stepchildren living together who are quite spread out in age. Would one of them be a suitable caregiver? Older teenagers may be ideal. Having a teenager care for your child during the summer may be an especially convenient arrangement. If your teenager is going to take care of your younger child, think of how she will be as a caregiver, not just as a babysitter. All-day, every-day care requires know-how.

If you do have a teenager care for your child, make sure she *is* old enough to take full responsibility for him. Some teenage girls become physically mature at an earlier age than others. This physical maturity is not necessarily related to any greater social maturity. You may have a thirteen-year-old who looks like an adult, but think twice before leaving her in charge of your two-year-old for the summer. Make sure that your teenager understands that you need a firm commitment for her services.

Father Care   When a father stays home and takes care of his child it really isn't day care, but it is an alternative. More fathers today are active, involved, and taking increasing pleasure in the day-to-day tasks associated with raising children. Research has shown that fathers can be just as responsive and stimulating for little babies as are mothers.

Natural childbirth organizations and the women's liberation movement should be credited with much of this trend toward shared parenting. More employers in general (though, sadly, not enough) and some professions in particular are becoming open to more flexible work schedules (called flex-time) that allow mothers and fathers to set their own hours and/or to work at home. (In Sweden, the government offers, and most families use, extensive, equal maternity and paternity leaves of absence from work.)

Unlike when she arranges day care with other family members, a mother will be making a mistake to feel she should be the boss in child-rearing decisions when the father is the caregiver. Each parent, and especially a father who has chosen the nontraditional role of primary caregiver, deserves an equal voice in deciding what the best ways are to raise his child.

Probably most day care by fathers is not the Monday-through-Friday, nine-to-five type of arrangement. (Sometimes it seems that every full-time house-husband in the United States has been written up at least once in some newspaper or magazine's "Family" or "Modern Living" section.) Yet the pattern is healthy, flourishing, and definitely catching on. In most father care arrangements, the mother works or goes to school evenings and/or weekends and the father takes over after he has put in a full day at work. But one family I know (both parents are M.D.'s) has arranged full-time father care during each day. The father works evenings in a hospital. Families who opt for a schedule that allows a lot of father care usually do it out of a strong desire for their child to grow up equally attached to both parents. Many such parents feel that equal sharing of the child care responsibilities, especially during the earliest months, is critical if this shared primary bond is going to develop. During this period the father and infant can have an opportunity to initiate lifelong bonds. In addition, it is often psychologically important for the mother to have some opportunity to get away from the house and reestablish her sense of individuality. Other families may want to use house-husbanding as a means for allowing a wife to continue with part-time work until both feel that the time is right for moving into a full-time day care arrangement outside of the home. For most families, however, the organization of the world of work will probably make it unrealistic to depend on fathers for day care on any long-term basis.

Live-in Caregivers   Some families choose to hire a caregiver who can live in. The decision to have a live-in caregiver is a major one, not only in terms of cost, but in terms of impact on your family structure. A couple should seriously consider how having another person living in the house will affect the intimacy of their family. Children are very tuned in to how real or artificial parental behavior is, and will respond with confusion and negativism if they sense that their parents' behavior is less than honest. If you can't be yourself with another person around, then a live-in caregiver may not be the right choice.

If your home is physically set up so that you and a caregiver can have separate spaces during those times your family may want to be alone, or for when she may want to be alone, then a live-in caregiver may work out well. It will be especially convenient if you have a special "maid's room," separate floor, or a detached cottage for your caregiver (unfortunately, not likely for city-dwellers).

Having a live-in caregiver was more common in the last century and in the early 1900s than it is today. These women were referred to as nannies or governesses. This nomenclature evokes images of ladies in starched uniforms with huge strollers perambulating through Central Park, or prim young women in wide skirts followed by numerous little ones across a multiacred lawn to the mansion.

In the less distant past, upper-middle-class families commonly were able to hire young, unmarried women whose passage to the United States from a South American or Caribbean country was sponsored in return for room, board, housework, child care, and a small salary. In recent years, new immigration laws and American monetary inflation have made this a less attractive alternative to prospective caregivers. It is also more difficult for families wishing to hire such caregivers. The Immigration and Naturalization Service (INS) and the U.S. Department of Labor (DOL) require you to do things such as advertise in your local paper and check the unemployment rolls before allowing you to bring in a non-American worker. More specifically, you will need a DOL certification before the INS will let you bring someone into the country. To get the proper DOL certification, you have to show that no unemployed American would want the job you have to offer. The INS is more sticky about this than they used to be, because of the recent influx of refugees and illegal aliens into the United States. Furthermore, you initially have to promise year-round employment to the prospective caregiver. But the INS regulations state that if things don't work out, you will be free to fire her.

Today, live-in caregivers are most often younger women from poorer families who find partial payment in the form of room and board an attractive proposition, especially in urban areas where the cost of living is high. Also, most of today's live-in caregivers function as general housekeepers, doing cleaning and shopping as well as child care.

This can be a very congenial arrangement. In-home care by a live-in caregiver is probably most suitable for those mothers who have large enough homes, can well afford it, and plan an early return to work, say, two to six weeks after the birth of the baby. If a live-in caregiver is to take care of a nearly newborn, it's advisable for her to arrive at least a week prior to your return to work. This will give you, her, and your baby a chance to get to know one another. Babies as young as four weeks old often can differentiate their mother's touch from that of other people. These very sensitive babies are apt to fuss at contact with a stranger. A breaking-in period will be needed.

The convenience of live-in help may appeal to you, but you may not need full-time assistance. An au pair may be just what you could use. An au pair girl is a young woman, often a student or someone just out of school, who wants to come to the United States for a year or so. Traditionally, au pairs have been Europeans (hence the French name). Some come to learn English or just to see the world. For room and board, they will provide at least part-time child care and maybe light housework. There are agencies in large cities that place au pairs. However, it is more difficult than in the past to arrange for an au pair because of immigration rules concerning who can and cannot officially work when visiting this country. If au pairs come as students, they will have an F-1 visa. This means that they must show that they will bring with them financial support from their own country. But students with F-1 visas are only allowed to work if they can show that they've developed an unforeseen economic necessity after entering the United States. On the other hand, if you arrange for an au pair to come as a domestic worker, you will have the same entry problems with the

DOL and INS as in hiring other non-American domestics. Visa and work permit problems aside, the greatest limitation to selecting an au pair is that you don't meet her until she comes. It is very difficult to judge the relative merits of prospective au pairs when you have such limited information in advance.

Daytime Housekeepers   While some housekeepers and au pairs live in, the majority of housekeepers "come in." Housekeepers are caregivers who come to your home, do housework, maybe cooking, and child care as well. Some daytime help do child care exclusively, or only housework that pertains directly to your children, for instance, cooking the children's meals, doing the children's laundry, cleaning up the path of devastation. Much of what has already been said about caregivers in general pertains to evaluating a housekeeper.

If you are going to have a daytime housekeeper, one major question will be how much housework she can do and still have time left for all your child's needs. Any working parent who has a housekeeper will tell you how glorious it is to come home to a clean house and cared-for children. Having help with housework may be especially nice during the first few months of your child's life, when you are still adjusting to parenthood as well as to the additional household chores a child creates. Even if you won't be able to afford to pay someone to do both housework and day care for the long run, having that luxury for those first few months may be well worth the expense.

Having a housekeeper as a short-term luxury is especially important if parenthood is not the bed of roses you quite expected and you feel that it is rough going. Many new mothers suffer from postpartum depression, sometimes called "the baby blues." A housekeeper can relieve just enough stress to give those feelings of being overwhelmed a chance to dissipate.

When your child is an infant, your housekeeper can clean while the baby sleeps. However, that stage of infancy, as you know, or will soon find out, is fleeting. Therefore, don't expect time dedicated to housework to exceed the time your child will be sleeping. Don't leave your housekeeper with several days of cleaning if you are only out of the house one or two days a week. When you come home, it will be very apparent what cleaning has and hasn't been done, but there is no certain way of telling how much time has been spent with your child. If you put great emphasis on how nice and clean the house is each time you arrive home, you will only be reinforcing the caregiver to spend more time doing housework and consequently leaving less time to pay attention to your child. Give at least equal play to a review of what the caregiver and child did together as to the cleanliness of your home. Tell your caregiver that her number-one priority is care of your child.

Share Care   One increasingly popular variant of in-home care is what I refer to as "share care." Share care is a cross between in-home care and family day care, where two to four families hire one in-home caregiver who cares for all the children together. The parents rotate homes where the care is given. Typically, each family offers its home for a few months at a time, so that each child has dual advantages of being somewhere familiar some of the time and somewhere novel at other times. Share care is a particularly nice arrangement for infants of nearly the same age.

Since the caregiver works for more than one family, she can receive a better salary than any one family would be likely to pay her. Usually, it's best if such caregivers only provide child care, no housework. Many feelings of inequity result if housework is done only for the host family. The trick with share care, as you probably sense, is finding a group with whom to share a caregiver. Chapter four will show you how child care referral agencies may be able to help you do this.

You will have most control over your child's care arrangement if you have one caregiver in your own home. Parents who opt for out-of-home care need to find caregivers and care settings that seem right, and subsequently monitor them and suggest modifications to the way their child is treated. Parents selecting out-of-home care often have less say over how things are managed, since other families and their child care needs are involved too. In any type of day care arrangement, you need to find someone whose good judgment you can absolutely trust.

Family Day Care Mothers

Caregivers who provide day care in their homes are referred to as family day care mothers or just day care mothers.

This is a very descriptive title, because that is exactly what this type of caregiver is: your child's "mother" while your child is in day care. She cares for, teaches, and loves your child when you're not available. Who a day care mother is, and what she is like as a person, have everything to do with how successful a family day care arrangement will be. She is the single most important element in day care quality. It's more important to find a family day care mother who is a good person than a family day care mother you could take or leave but who has wonderful toys, lives near a beautiful park, or even has a wonderful group of other kids. As far as finding a family day care mother that you will personally get along with, much of what has been said about selecting in-home caregivers with the right "chemistry" applies.

The vast majority of family day care mothers may be described in one of two ways: they are either mothers of preschool-age children themselves, or older women with kids who are in school all day or who are grown up. Seldom will you meet a day care mother who has either not yet had children of her own, or who has never been a mother. Most of the younger family day care mothers stay home and do day care because they want to be with their own children, but still need to contribute to the family income. The younger family day care mothers usually plan to go back to work or school "someday" when their children are grown or when their husbands have established their careers. Most older day care mothers have never worked outside the home, or at least not since they've been married. Running a household and child-raising are what they like to do best and know that they can do best. Like younger family day care mothers, these women often are working because they need to contribute to their family's income.

Many family day care mothers are unaware that their work is part of a larger social network of women who do just what they do and who, as a group, provide a very widely used form of day care. Often, they just don't know what a valuable community resource they are. A family day care mother may refer to herself as a sitter.

If you call one on the phone and ask if she is a family day care mother, she may say "huh?" Then, if you ask whether she babysits, she will say yes. (On the other hand, there are those who, if asked whether they are babysitters, will indignantly reply, "No, I'm a family day care mother.")

Some family day care mothers think of themselves as providers of some kind of social welfare; that they are helping out a poor young woman (you), who has to work. If you or your spouse harbors any militant feelings toward those who express such views, stay away. It's just that sort of attitude that can start a day care arrangement off on the wrong foot. Other day care mothers figure that you are doing what you want to be doing (working), and that they are doing what they want to be doing (staying home), and that both are OK. A family day care mother (especially a younger one) may be sensitive to the fact that you spend your day in the "real" world, while she spends her days at home in Munchkinland with little adult contact.

Often family day care mothers are "homebodies." They like to cook, seem to mind cleaning less than most of us, and don't feel too homebound if they only get out of the house to go to the grocery store and do the nursery-school carpool.

Family day care mothers tend to be moderately educated. Most have finished high school, but fewer have finished college. As a group, they are better educated than in-home caregivers. This is a noteworthy point because research has repeatedly shown a strong relation between a mother's level of education and the early achievements of her child. While there is debate on how much of this phenomenon is due to environment and how much is due to heredity, it is clear that more highly educated mothers use a more open, less authoritarian teaching style. This finding is largely independent of what the mother has been educated to do. Therefore, it's relevant to consider how well educated a caregiver is, since this can be expected to relate to how effectively she structures your child's learning experiences.

It is important to evaluate how well you and a prospective day care mother agree on issues related to child-rearing. A study of parent-caregiver relations made in Portland, Oregon, found that when parents and family day care mothers shared child-rearing values, there was greater mutual satisfaction with the day care arrangement, and the arrangements lasted significantly longer.

Day Care Center Caregivers

The approach that must be taken when assessing caregivers in a day care center is necessarily very different from assessments of in-home caregivers or of family day care mothers. This is because your child will be influenced by a group of caregivers rather than by a single person. It is necessary to evaluate each individual caregiver to a degree, as well as to evaluate how the staff operates as a team.

Most day care centers have four levels of staff. The director coordinates all the staff activity, performs administrative duties, and is responsible for the daily structure, or programming. Directors usually have at least two years of work experience with children, either in day care or in schools. Most have B.A. degrees in education or psychology, or in lieu of that, many more years of experience. In many "educational" or "developmental" centers, the director may have an M.A. in education, or specialized post-college training in child care or early childhood education. However, as a minimum requirement, most states call only for day care center directors to be high school graduates and "show interest in working with children." Former elementary-school teachers often turn up as day care center directors.

Head teachers and teachers are at the second and third levels of staffing. (In most centers, these caregivers are called teachers, so I will use that term to describe them, even though I prefer *caregiver* for reasons stated earlier.) Head teachers and teachers tend to be fairly young. Most are not yet parents themselves. There is typically one head teacher per room or age group. The head teacher reports directly to the director. She is responsible for keeping things running smoothly for her group. She moves the children from one activity to the next, sees to it that the appropriate toys and materials are available, and helps the staff spread out among the children. The head teacher is the major role model for less experienced staff members. In many centers, the head teacher has the closest daily contact with parents. It is her responsibility to report on difficulties the child may be experiencing while at the center. In many small day care centers (under sixty children), the director works part of her time as head teacher. The head teacher is usually the most senior caregiver in the room. It is often the head teacher's job to serve as liaison between other staff and the director, settling disputes among staff before their behavior with the children is affected negatively. This is especially true in large day care centers with many (say, ten or more) classrooms. In larger centers, the head teacher becomes more of an administrator and less of a caregiver.

The educational training requirements for head teachers and teachers vary from state to state. Some states have no minimum requirement. In most states, the prerequisite is a high school diploma. In a few states, a post–high school Child Development Associate (CDA) certificate or its equivalent is required. (Teachers and directors often have the same amounts of formal training but directors typically have a good deal of hands-on experience as well.)

Pay for working in a day care center is usually poor, comparable to working in a department store, or at another job that one associates with many fewer responsibilities than are involved in caring for young children. Caregivers in centers are often paid minimun wage. It's really a sad statement about our society's values. It also can make it difficult for centers to attract and retain well-qualified staff.

The fourth level of staffing is teachers' aides. Teachers' aides are a more heterogeneous group than are higher-level staff. Aides may be regular full-time caregivers who can't be distinguished from the teachers; some are students who are doing a practicum for education or child-development classes; parent co-op centers use parent volunteers as aides; sometimes, senior citizens volunteer, or are employed to give children exposure to older adults. Staff turnover is typically highest for aides. They have a lot of tasks delegated to them, and are, needless to say, even more poorly paid than are teachers, if they are paid at all. Aides spend a lot of time carrying out routine activities, such as wiping kids down after meals, doing diaper or potty patrol, setting up for meals and cleaning up afterward. However, when tasks like this are out of the way, aides are freer to spend extended periods of time with one or two children. They don't have the administrative duties that other staff do.

Now that you know the essentials of staff structure, you need a little background on the relative importance of each of these roles.

The day care center director, unless she is the head teacher as well, will be least likely to have extended contact with your child. If you don't like her style, but like what you see in the center, fine. If she's good at administrative tasks, that may be what's most important, especially in a larger center.

The head teacher tends to be the most stable, constantly available person. Aides tend to come and go during the day while she stays. Children tend to relate most strongly to the person they can most depend on to be there. Another reason the head teacher plays a central role is that she is the one most likely to step in if there's been a fight, or if a child is sick or has been hurt. Children tend to gravitate to those who help them during emotional crises. The head teacher also sets the tone or attitude toward work that the other teachers and aides will reflect.

All of the care, instruction, and attention that the head teacher may provide for your child may just as likely be provided by other teachers in the room. Many times the head teacher is indistinguishable as she moves among her staff and among the children. There's nothing inherently wrong with that. It usually means things are well run.

Your child will probably find one caregiver — an aide, a teacher, or the head teacher — who is her favorite, just because of that person's willingness to give your child some special time. The things that person does with him will be especially important. If you help foster the development of that relationship, you'll be helping your child feel more at ease in the day care center.

Caregiver–Child Ratio   The number of caregivers compared to the number of children (caregiver–child ratio) is a very important consideration. Researchers from the National Day Care Study showed that the more children per caregiver, the more time spent controlling children, rather than teaching or playing with them. This study also found that a group size of fifteen to eighteen children or less encouraged better caregiving for three- to five-year-olds, even if there was a sufficient number of caregivers for a larger group. For children under three years old, actual caregiver-to-child ratio made the difference. These findings showed that it was important to have small classes and, for very young children, many teachers, as well.

Parent Co-ops   Some day care centers are run as parent cooperatives, a popular means of keeping the caregiver-to-child ratio high, while keeping costs low. Typically, parents pay a reduced fee, and volunteer time about two half-days per month. (Fee reductions and volunteer time depend on the size of the center, age of the children, numbers of full-paying families, and so on.)

One real advantage of well-run parent co-ops is that they provide the parents (who have the time) with an alternative perspective on who their child is; that is, how he fits in as a member of a peer group. Some parent co-ops provide formal or informal channels for parents to learn about child development. For example, parents may have evening group meetings to learn more about the mechanics of the program or the teaching philosophy of the staff. (Other centers that are not co-ops may have similar parent programs that allow you to observe, though not participate.) If you don't make observations of your child while co-oping, it is important to take special time periodically to do so. It's particularly nice if the center has a one-way mirror or other vantage point where parents can watch without the child reacting to the fact that the parents are observing.

When I go to a day care center I am seldom impressed positively by parent volunteers as caregivers. First of all, I can pick them out, right away. The parent volunteer is playing awkwardly with one child, while another (his own child) clings to his leg. I call this the "parents-as-warm-bodies-in-the-room" approach to volunteer staffing. Parent volunteers usually don't have enough familiarity with all the minutiae of the routine, and children really derive a lot of security from that routine. Parent volunteers often don't know the children's names. Most parent co-ops I've seen require the kids to keep name tags pinned on. That's awfully depersonalizing. Worse, children less than three years old or so have a hard time understanding why Mommy is here today, and not tomorrow. It is difficult for them to develop a clear set of expectations about what does and does not go on in day care, and why they have to share Mommy with the other children sometimes. One creative solution to this problem has been achieved by a co-op day care center in Toronto. Parents of these young children contribute their hours in a classroom with children older than their own. This way, the younger children do not become anxious about sharing their parents, or about the parents' comings and goings. By being with older children, the parents get a taste of what it will be like when their own children are a little older.

DAY CARE ENVIRONMENTS

Caregivers contribute a great deal to the success of a day care arrangement. If I were forced to give it a number, I would say that caregivers make 75 percent of the difference in whether a day care arrangement is a good one or not. The other 25 percent of the success or failure would be due to the day care environment. Day care environment is a term meant to encompass the physical environment (the rooms, their layout, the toys, the outdoor space); the program or routine; and peer influences. These components of day care determine what your child's cognitive and social surroundings will be like. In some cases, a truly amazing variety of toys (or the absolute lack of them), or a very close relationship with another child (or the presence of a hyperaggressive one), might positively or negatively color a whole day care experience. Most of the time, however, these factors do not seem to be as overwhelmingly important as the characteristics of the caregivers.

What's It Like for a Child to Be at Home All Day?

If you are going to have an in-home child care arrangement, you should rate how suitable your home will be as a day care environment. How does it compare to other places in which a child is cared for? Is it a place where your child can be all day without getting bored or feeling confined? For example, if you live in a stu-

dio apartment, you will want to think twice before arranging for
in-home care. Children (except of course very tiny babies, who
don't stay that way for very long) need physical space, as well as
toys, to be happily active. The environment should not be overly
restrictive. Your home should be child-proof, so you don't have to
worry about physical dangers while you're away. Most of the space
should be accessible to your child's play. While it is good for your
child to learn that some things are off limits, you don't want to set
up a situation where constant reprimands are needed.

One obvious advantage of in-home care is that the child need
not leave his own, familiar home and adjust to strange surroundings. Especially for children under one year of age, being around
familiar sights may be nearly as important as being around parents
and siblings. Information that has been provided by psychologists
who study how infants learn to think (notably, the Swiss psychologist Jean Piaget) suggests that *schemes* (familiar sights and patterns
of events) are important building blocks for intellectual development.

It is quite natural to want to find in-home care for your very
young child. If you feel that your child is particularly in need of
the type of comfort that is offered by the stability of being in his
own home, you have all the more reason to consider in-home care.
You really shouldn't worry that in-home care gives a child less to
do than out-of-home care. The normal activities of the home —
cooking, cleaning, gardening, shopping, talking on the phone, and
so forth — all provide a young child with educational experiences.
They are learning the social order of things. On the other hand,
when the caregiver plays directly with your child — doing puzzles,
reading books, counting, stacking blocks — those are educational
experiences too, but of a different nature. This first type of educational experience can be described as adult-oriented activities. The
second type of educational experience involves doing what the
child initiates, and can be called child-oriented activities.

In-home care, family day care, and center day care can be compared in terms of how adult- or child-oriented each environment
is. The relative amounts of adult- versus child-oriented activities
occurring in an in-home arrangement depend upon what the care-

giver's role is. If the caregiver is the grandmother who goes about her daily life — doing household chores, visiting friends, and such — and attends to your child when necessary, the environment will be fairly adult-oriented. Your child would be exposed more to the world of adults than to the world of other children. If you choose to hire someone who only cares for your child, and has no housekeeping responsibilities, or if you opt for share care, your child will receive a lot of attention. In other words, your home will provide a very child-oriented environment.

What's It Like to Be in Family Day Care All Day?

Family day care usually falls in the middle of the range from adult to child orientation of the environment. The family day care mother typically spends some time with children and some time doing household chores. In my research, I showed that family day care mothers spend essentially the same amount of time inter-acting with children as mothers do. The difference was that family day care mothers are spreading that same amount of time over more children. This suggests that the more children there are in a day care home, the less individualized the care will be.

The physical environment of a day care home is one of a private home. Some day care mothers rearrange their homes a great deal to accommodate their child care arrangements; others don't rear-range anything, allowing the children to have the run of the house or apartment. Many times, one main playroom has been set aside: a family room, a downstairs playroom, a Florida room, an extra bedroom, even the living room. The children's toys are located mainly in that room. There may be a TV there for the children to watch, particularly shows like *Sesame Street, Mister Rogers' Neighborhood,* or *Electric Company.* (Contrary to some uninformed opinions, young children don't even care to watch soap operas or game shows.) The main playroom is usually adjacent to the kitchen or somewhere the day care mother can do things on her own some of the time but still be within earshot.

Many day care mothers purchase child-size table and chairs for sedentary play activities and mealtimes. Others have special items for younger babies, like walkers and jolly jump-ups. There are usually many more toys than in any one child's home.

A small proportion of families use a day care home arrangement where the day care mother isn't caring for any other children. In that case, the arrangement is very much like having an in-home arrangement except that it isn't your own home. But most family day care mothers take care of three or four children. A small number care for ten or more. Depending on the number of children, the routine will be more or less rigid. When there are more children, a set schedule is often used, and the activities tend to be more child-oriented than when there are fewer children. A typical day in family day care begins with indoor activities in the morning, frequently accompanied by educational TV. Most day care mothers do not see TV as an activity in itself, but rather something to take up the slack as kids move from one toy to the next. Sometimes TV is an interim activity until all the children have arrived. Day care mothers who planned one or two structured activities per day, such as music, cooking, or arts and crafts, tend to do it in the morning when the children are most fresh. After mid-morning snacks, the routine usually includes outdoor play, weather permitting. As all experienced caregivers know, plenty of fresh air makes little children hungry and sleepy, so when they come in, the kids eat lunch and take naps or have quiet time. The afternoon includes more play, and sometimes more group activities. The rest of the afternoon may include a carpool run, or errands, or staying around the house having snacks, playing some more, and watching the second round of educational TV programs in the afternoon. In many day care homes, after-school-care kids begin to arrive around 3:00, providing a change of pace for the younger ones.

This routine can vary considerably depending on the ages of the children in the group. Older, nursery-school-age children who are cared for together tend to spend time in more structured activities, and participate more in group times. If there are mostly children under three, the free-play atmosphere is more pervasive. Children also seem to benefit from a mixed age group. Age mixing occurs quite naturally in family day care, far more than in centers. In my own research on play behavior in family day care, more mature forms of play with peers was related to the presence of an age-mixed group. Chicago-based researchers examined studies of nursery schools and similarly concluded that age mixing is better than age segregation because in age-segregated groups, there is less affection and more competitiveness between children.

It is typical for children under three years old to spend little time really interacting with other children. There is more parallel play than interactive play. Parallel play means that the children play with similar toys at similar times, glancing at one another occasionally, but never really talk or cooperate.

The overall quality of these characteristics of the family day care environment will be greatly affected by how much the caregiver is actively involved in teaching and facilitating the activities and the interactions among the children.

There are generally three categories of family day care: unlicensed homes, licensed homes, and network or sponsored homes. In some areas of the country (Texas, for example), there are also registered homes, as well as licensed ones.

"Licensed" probably sounds like a better thing to you than "unlicensed." Wrong. In fact, it means very, very little. An unlicensed home is one that is not recognized by any government agency. The day care mother has simply filed no official forms about her occupation. A licensed day care mother ("provider," in bureaucratese) has received a state permit to take care of a certain number of children (usually six) and has had the physical environment of her home deemed safe by a county inspector who looked for loose wires and exposed, rusty nails. Licensing in some states includes fingerprinting, a check for a record of criminal child abuse, a chest X ray, and a TB test. No one even tries to judge whether the day care mother has any innate ability to care for children adequately.

Licensing is no assurance of the quality of care! Don't let a family day care mother tell you that her license means that she is a better caregiver than someone without a license. She didn't have to pass any test, take any course, or do anything else to prove that she is competent to take care of children well. I can't begin to count the number of parents I've encountered who think that a license is like a degree, and that it must in some way guarantee a better quality of care. The reason that most family day care mothers get a license is that they feel it will attract parents. In fact, it entitles them to referral by public child care agencies, and makes them eligible for government fees that subsidize the costs of day care for some children. Among the day care mothers I've known, I'd guess that only 10 percent have been licensed. Many don't even know that there is such a thing as family day care licensing.

Some states register (simply take the name and address of) family day care mothers, and provide their names for referral, thus leaving parents more choice. I strongly favor this system over licensing.

Family day care mothers who belong to networks sometimes have to meet certain child development–related qualifications. These networks are groups of family day care mothers who work collaboratively, often sharing referrals, toys, sick days, days off, and other resources. Many networks serve a particular group of people, such as members of a university community (Yale University has such a network). Family day care mothers who are sponsored by a network sometimes participate in ongoing training.

A second nationwide study of day care was commissioned by the federal government to study family day care. That study, the National Day Care Home Study, asked whether unlicensed, licensed, or network day care homes were better.

Briefly, they found that the best care was provided by network homes and, in general, that the quality of care in unlicensed and licensed homes was the same, but somewhat lower than for network homes. The differences in quality when licensed and unlicensed care were compared were related to how much education the caregiver had received; that is, all education, not just child development. Unlicensed day care mothers tended to be somewhat less educated than licensed ones. Unlicensed day care mothers also tended to care for fewer children than licensed ones, and therefore had more time to spend with each child.

What's It Like to Be at a Day Care Center All Day?

The daily routine at a day care center is much like the routine in a day care home, except on a larger scale. Many day care centers for children three years old and older are run as nursery school programs, or there is a nursery school program in the morning and day care in the afternoon.

A world of difference exists between day care centers and nursery schools. *Nursery school* implies a curriculum with instructional goals that are related to gaining preacademic skills. Strictly speaking, day care centers are different because they are places where children learn informally from the experiences that they have with adults, children, and play materials around them. Of course, some facilities provide a combination of these services; for example, morning nursery school and afternoon day care.

It is dangerous for parents to be deluded into automatically equating day care with school, because of all the positive and beneficial outcomes we associate with school attendance. Some day care centers refer to themselves as schools and some parents refer to these day care centers as schools. When day care centers do this, it implies something they are probably not delivering. For parents, it provides a false sense that their child is getting an academic preparation when he may not be. The misnomer of "school" is especially annoying when applied to infant and toddler day care centers, where children are too young for any developmentally appropriate formal instruction. Such instruction in infant day care centers is not likely to be different from a home-based caregiver's caregiving.

One way of categorizing day care centers is by their sponsorship. There are three main categories of sponsorship for centers. Probably most prevalent are the private, nonprofit centers. These take many forms: parent cooperatives, industry-based centers (open to children of employees, and sometimes the adjacent community), church-run centers, university or college-run centers (open to members of the academic community), and those run by service organizations such as the YMCA.

A second type of sponsorship for day care centers is public: state, county, or school-district supported. Most public centers receive some federal, as well as state, funds, and are the most stringently regulated type of day care center. In the past, centers that wanted to be eligible for federal subsidies had to comply with a set of federal regulations for day care called FIDCR (Federal Inter-Agency Day Care Requirements). FIDCR was more strict about the caregiver–child ratio, provision of free meals, and caregiver training than were many state day care regulatory agencies. In the mid-1970s, the federal government commissioned a multimillion-dollar review of FIDCR that resulted in improved standards for day care centers. But as part of its federal deregulation policy, the Reagan Administration threw out these regulations before they were ever implemented. Now states can fall back on their own, often less demanding, regulations, and still qualify for federal subsidy of day care programs. It remains to be seen just how much of a step backward the elimination of FIDCR will be for day care quality. In the past, public centers frequently offered the best-quality care. Because of the federal deregulation, I would expect private, nonprofit centers (which were never far behind) to take the lead.

The third type of day care center is the private, run-for-profit center. These centers are run by individuals or corporations (franchises) as money-making ventures. I have never seen a franchised run-for-profit infant or toddler program that I felt was truly good. Further, no day care professional I trust has ever told me about one, nor have I ever read about one in any reliable source. As far as I'm concerned, it's not possible to provide good-quality care for children under three and still make a corporation-sized profit. One critic of run-for-profit day care coined the phrase "Kentucky Fried Children" in reference to these chains of day care centers. There are, however, many good run-for-profit programs for children three years old and older.

In addition, a fourth, rather uncommon, source of day care sponsorship is the U.S. military. I've only been to one military-run day care center and it was the worst, most unsupervised day care I've ever seen. (The parents never saw the center, because they passed their children over a counter by the entrance.) Even though they are run by the government, military-base centers are subject to no day care regulations, not even FIDCR.

Sponsorship is just a rough predictor of a day care center's quality standards. Profit-making status is certainly a better indicator, especially when considering day care for very young children.

All day care centers provide informal learning experiences that are facilitated by caregivers whose job it is to help children get the most out of their own experiences. The way in which caregivers go about "teaching" has a lot to do with how a program is run. You can think of caregiver teaching styles along a continuum from laissez-faire to authoritarian. The laissez-faire caregiver sits at the table with the crayons and paper and waits for a child to ask her to draw a horse. The authoritarian caregiver gathers a group of children, sits them around the table, hands out crayons and paper, and tells them to draw horses. If the child draws something else, the caregiver says, "We're drawing horses today, not spaceships." Laissez-faire caregivers allow the child to initiate the learning sequence on a topic of his choice. A caregiver with a more authoritarian orientation will initiate a learning sequence of her choosing, based on what she feels will be most beneficial for the child. Realistically, most day care programs fall somewhere along this continuum, rather than at either end. The type of program you choose should be one that complements your own parenting style with your child. One method is not inherently better than another for all children.

Another way to assess a day care program is to determine whether it is "open" or "closed." An open program is one in which there is a low level of routine, with emphasis usually placed on social development rather than formal learning. A closed program is one where there is a set curriculum to be covered, and learning objectives are emphasized more than socialization and self-expression. Again, most programs fall somewhere along this continuum, and selection depends on your preferences and goals for your child.

Yet another way of describing day care programs has to do with the fact that everything is going on for the children's benefit: the child-oriented/adult-oriented distinction made earlier. Center day care is the most child-oriented form of day care. The adults have no other duties except those (directly or indirectly) related to the children. Studies of day care done in Sweden and Massachusetts both reported that caregivers in day care centers were less controlling than family day care mothers or mothers at home — perhaps because center caregivers have fewer responsibilities in addition to child care. However, there are fewer adults per child in day care centers than in other forms of day care, so each child tends to receive less individual attention from caregivers.

Is it better for day care to be child-oriented or adult-oriented? There is no clear answer. Critics of in-home care arrangements and of family day care point out that the child is secondary to what the adult needs to accomplish in order to keep her daily routine afloat. Critics of center day care point out that these children do not have enough "real world" experiences; that they gain the unrealistic impression that the world revolves around them, and their pursuit of interesting things to do. I think that both of these views are partly valid and partly extreme. A day care environment that exposes children to the world of adults, as well as allocating time for activities expressly for the child, seems to be the best solution. Good day care centers plan field trips just to get the kids out of the center and into the goings-on of their communities. Some centers make it a practice for caregivers to take one or two kids along whenever they go out for groceries or on other errands.

Usually a day care center has one room per age group. The room is divided into different activity areas, such as block-building, reading, housekeeping toys (dolls, sinks and stoves, for example), and fine-motor-skill toys. Most centers have child-size tables and chairs for eating and crafts activities. There is usually a series of cubbies or bins for each child's personal belongings. (One center uses empty ten-gallon bins from an ice cream store for this purpose.) In good weather, many centers let children wander between inside and out, with some caregivers in each place. Like school classrooms, day care centers hang up things the kids have made, and have seasonal theme bulletin boards for the walls. Parent sign-in/sign-out charts and nap/feeding schedules cover other walls.

Children with similar interests can group together in the story corner to listen to the caregiver who is reading, or go over to the caregiver who is helping kids cooperate to build a castle out of blocks. At least one caregiver is usually circulating, picking up toys that kids are finished with, wiping noses, taking children to the potty, greeting parents as they bring their children.

Research on Children in Day Care Centers   The most comprehensive review of day care research, published in 1978, summarizing numerous studies, noted that children who attended day care were more aggressive, less cooperative with adults, and showed less enthusiasm for educational activities once they started school. An example of a study that produced findings like these was completed by researchers at Syracuse University. They reported this pattern of negative behavior in five-year-olds who, as infants, had attended a very high-quality model day care program at their college.

Research on children in day care has produced variable, sometimes conflicting, results. The main feature of day care centers that is different from home-based forms of care is that children are in constant contact with many other children. One study comparing children in day care centers to children at home found that children in centers were more competent at playing with peers. In a recent study that I coauthored, we confirmed those findings but also showed that the cost of learning to play with others was more fighting among children in centers than is usual among children at home or in family day care.

Although some professionals have reported negative effects of attending day care centers, many others have found no such effects when comparing children attending different types of day care. There are many reasons for their disagreements. Some examined very high-quality day care; some, very low-quality day care. Some studied the children of the poor; others, the children of the highly educated. The methods used in some studies were imprecise, and of questionable accuracy.

It is difficult to compare different types of day care because they can overlap so much. A day-care home with ten children and a teenage helper can look more like a day care center than a day care center with an enrollment of twelve and one adult for every four children. An in-home arrangement with three siblings together will look more like family day care than a family day care home with only one child.

Finally, the kind of care that one set of parents wants for their child is the kind of care another set of parents would never opt for in a million years. What any one of us considers to be high quality is to some extent subjective, and depends upon an individual's values.

Giving Your Child a Balanced Variety of Social Experiences   For children who go to day care, time spent in parks, playgrounds, and other fun places allows them to become familiar with the world that exists outside their daily routine. One thing that I worry about when it comes to children who are in day care all day, five days a week, is this: parents get their dose of out-of-home excitement while at work, so when the parents are home, they want to enjoy that, and the peace of being alone with their family. If the child doesn't get out much during day care hours, and doesn't get out much when the parents are home, the child may be living in quite a narrow environment that simply cannot reflect the full texture of the world around him.

During nonworking hours, parents can compensate and supplement the child- and adult-oriented experiences that occur in the day care environment. Since parents do many things, see different people, and travel to different places during their working hours, it can be difficult for them to realize that their child's physical environment is relatively static during those times. If your child is at home, or at her day care mother's all week, make a special effort to get out of the house on the weekends so that your child will have a change of scenery. If your child is in a day care center all week, encourage her to follow you around the house; explain your activities to her as you go. Take her places as well. The environment your child experiences in day care and the environment you create for your child during your nonworking hours should provide a blend of people, places, and things.

Practical Considerations That May Influence Your Choice of Child Care

EVERY FAMILY CAN BE EXPECTED to want the best possible day care that it can find. Realistically, there are always practical constraints imposed upon your ability to find an ideal day care arrangement. These constraints may be related to where you live, where you work, what you can afford to spend, and what kind of day care is already established in your community. You are bound to have a difficult time when you try to weigh possible benefits to your child against definite convenience to you. You need to compare apples and oranges. There is no scientific, right way to do this. The best caveat is neither to ignore what may be better for your child in favor of the most readily available, least expensive day care; nor to go overboard and opt for a fancy-named child development center a half hour from your house, another half hour from your job, and costing $150 week.

The four major topics that you will want to consider when evaluating the convenience of each type of care arrangement are:

- *location* of the day care arrangement
- *flexibility* of days and hours that day care can be scheduled
- *availability of the necessary paraphernalia of child-rearing:* baby foods, baby furniture, clothes, and diapers
- *cost* of day care.

LOCATION

A good rule of thumb is that you should find a day care arrangement that is within five to ten minutes of your route to work. This formula should work, regardless of the form of transportation that you use to get to your job or whether you live in a city or a suburb. Besides the time you take to get to the day care arrangement, you'll also need to allow drop-off and pick-up time.

When you have an in-home care arrangement, obviously you don't have to take your child anywhere. This can be a real advantage in the care of infants where a great deal of paraphernalia accompanies each foray from the home. If transportation between your home and your work is problematic (for example, you have to take a train, two buses, and a subway), leaving your child at home may make your life a lot easier. One drawback to having your day care arrangement located in your own home has to do with where your home is situated. It's nice to have your child within easy distance of a park or play area. Another nice thing to have is contact with some other children the same age who live nearby.

Day care homes tend to be located in residential areas, since they are themselves homes. If you work in a downtown area and commute, you will be more likely to find day care near where you live than where you work.

Sometimes it can be emotionally difficult, knowing that your child is not where you can get to her easily. Think about how the distance from your child will make you feel. You may find that you feel strongly about using a type of care that is near your work.

Day care centers, as opposed to day care homes, are more likely to be close to places of work. Many day care centers are located on large residential thoroughfares. Since churches, former elementary schools, community centers, YMCAs, and the like are favorite sites for day care centers, you're apt to find day care centers wherever these places are located in your city or town. A tiny minority of enlightened industries have tried to operate day care centers located at their facilities for their employees. (In Massachusetts, companies such as KLH and Stride-Rite developed model programs that have received national recognition.) Hospitals are prominent among institutions employing large numbers of women that sponsor day care centers. Day care centers are sometimes based within a housing project. Depending on the size of the project, one apartment per building may be set aside for use as a day care center.

SCHEDULING FLEXIBILITY

Day care arrangements vary a great deal in terms of the flexibility you may have in day-to-day and week-to-week scheduling changes.

In-home day care may be the best choice if you work mostly during hours when other people don't. If you work a night shift or a swing shift, someone at home may be able to provide you with day care. An in-home care arrangement may also be most convenient for the mother of more than one child. If you have three children, for example, and the one-year-old has Kinder-Gym Monday morning, and the three-year-old has nursery school Tuesday and Thursday afternoons, and your six-year-old has ballet Wednesday and Friday after school, then an in-home caregiver who picks up, delivers, and is home at all the right times may be your only hope. If you are a physician and are on call every third twenty-four-hour period, in-home care may be the only way you can drop everything and run.

Family day care is usually the next most flexible type of care in terms of available hours. I've known some day care mothers (with husbands who work early shifts) who take children as early as 5:30 A.M. (In one case, the child's mother catered breakfasts. This little boy arrived in his pajamas around 5:00 A.M., finished sleeping at his day care mother's house, and later got up with the rest of her family at about 7:30 A.M.) When you plan on working unusual hours, you should consider how your child will take to it, as well as how you'll manage. For the most part, family day care children arrive after breakfast, between 8:00 A.M. and 9:00 A.M., and stay until around 5:15 P.M. to 6:30 P.M.

Some day care centers are open long hours: 6:00 A.M. to 8:00 P.M. However, most have hours like 8:00 A.M. to 6:00 P.M. A few centers keep hours that are more like a preschool's (9:00 A.M. to

5:00 P.M.). Some preschools offer extended-day care; that is, day care before and after each day's preschool component.

Often, a few caregivers come early or stay late each day while the rest work eight-hour days in between. Some centers that keep longer hours and have full attendance much of the time employ two separate shifts of caregivers. Some centers have a separate night shift. One center I used to visit was open until midnight. This was a big help to its largely single mother clientele. These mothers sometimes worked during the day and went to school in the evenings, or worked night shifts so they could be at home with their children during the day.

Centers tend to be stricter than family day care mothers about sticking to the agreed-upon hours. Many charge double time or double time plus a late fee if you are more than fifteen minutes late or past closing time. Some centers will charge as much as two dollars for every five minutes you are late. Some late fee policies seem overly punitive but they really have to do this, because their staff have families and lives outside their jobs, too. Centers typically charge you for a full day, even if you pick your child up earlier than expected. Similarly, you may be expected to pay for sick days. They must do this, because they have reserved their time for your child.

Some people need day care for different numbers of hours each week — students, for example. Other people have business schedules that include numerous meetings of indeterminate length. Still others have to work a fixed number of hours each week sometime between 8:00 A.M. on Monday and 6:00 P.M. on Friday. Some, such as doctors and nurses, may not be working full-time, but may be intermittently on call. If you need different numbers of hours each day, or different numbers of hours each week, or drop-in flexibility, consider the following.

If in-home care is provided by a live-in relative or housekeeper, you will have the most flexibility. You can come and go as you wish. You won't have to call anyone to see if she is free to come now. You won't have to drive anyone crazy with a weekly thirty-minute lecture on what your schedule for the coming week will be. (An arrangement like that invites slip-ups, missed connections, and raised tempers.) However, hardly anyone can arrange and/or afford a full-time on-call caregiver if they are not working full-time.

If you can't possibly have a live-in arrangement, but you need drop-in care, the advantage of in-home convenience for your schedule is lost. If you have to wait until you can reach your caregiver, and wait for her to come over to your place, then you might as well be using that time to take your child somewhere where you can "drop-in" anytime.

A family day care mother may be the next best thing to a live-in caregiver if you need drop-in care. Most day care mothers are home a large proportion of the time. A day care mother will usually like a rough idea of when you may be coming and going (for example, early morning, late morning, after lunch, after nap). Often day care mothers juggle the schedules of a number of part-time children, and just want to be sure that everyone won't be there at once. If you need day care for, say, three days a week, you'll be more likely to find a day care home where you can pick *which* three days. This is more difficult to arrange with centers where part-time, three days a week, usually means Monday, Wednesday, Friday. Also, centers tend to reserve openings for those in need of full-time care.

If your hours will be changing over the months to come (say you're returning to work two days a week with plans to increase to full time over the next several months), then a family day care arrangement will probably be most adaptable to those conditions.

Day care centers usually have less leeway for drop-in care than do home-based care arrangements. Day care centers are responsible to their licensing agencies never to exceed a certain caregiver-to-child ratio. Because of this, it is impossible for most centers to offer drop-in care unless they specifically allocate slots for drop-ins as part of their calculated ADA (average daily attendance). Most centers choose not to do this, because if no children drop in, they lose funds that they have counted on to pay staff.

Some communities have specially established drop-in care facilities. Typically, these centers are used by women who do not work, but just want a "sanity break" once or twice a week. Centers that specialize in serving drop-in kids just can't provide a stable enough environment, stable enough routine, or staff to be suitable for those who need day care more often.

BABY PARAPHERNALIA AND FEEDING_____

The amount of child paraphernalia needed on a trip away from home is inversely proportional to the size of the child. For those who'd like a less mathematical restatement: infants are constantly surrounded by the many conveniences of modern child-rearing. By preschool age, cradles, cribs, high chairs, walkers, jump seats, formulas, baby food, endless changes of clothes, diapers, potties, and other instruments of infant torture have been left in the dust. (Those of you with small babies may find this hard to believe!)

How much of this paraphernalia will you provide and how much of it will be provided as part of the day care arrangement? Obviously, with in-home care, you provide whatever you feel is necessary. Day-care centers will be equipped with essential baby hardware, such as changing tables, porto-cribs, cots, and high chairs. Federal, state, and local health and safety codes specify the minimum number of these items for a given group of children, as well as the space that the equipment must have. These regulations vary somewhat from locale to locale. For example, in some counties, sleeping areas may have to be separate from play areas, with cots three feet apart. In other places, children may bring mats from home and sleep on the floor of the main playroom. Most day care centers tend not to have large numbers of the less vital baby hardware, such as walkers, infant seats, and indoor baby swings. All the better. If you do find a day care center with a row of ten infant bounce seats, beware! That sort of thing is the hallmark of routinized, nonindividualized care. At centers, little ones are placed on carpets or blankets on the floor in an enclosed area during times when they're not being directly played with. A couple of day care centers I've seen have had huge (10' x 10') elevated playpens so that the infants could crawl and roll without being trod upon by toddlers!

In family day care, the day care mother is often the mother of young children herself. In this case, she will have much of the

needed baby hardware. Other, older day care mothers have accumulated these things over the years of having their own kids and
taking care of other people's kids. Because they do day care, they
tend to "inherit" baby hardware from friends.

Sometimes, the day care mother will not have everything you
need. It may be that her own child still uses the high chair. Or she
may not have previously taken children who are young enough to
need to sleep in a crib. It would certainly be more convenient to
find a day care mother who has all the baby equipment that you
need, but that should not be a main criterion for selecting her. You
can encourage a prospective caregiver to get the needed equipment. Or you can purchase it yourself. (Splitting the cost is probably not a good idea, since one of you will end up keeping it.) An
alternative might be for her to buy one item, and you to buy another. Other mothers using the same day care arrangement might
be willing to lend the day care mother something that you need.
One good way to get extra equipment is to go to garage sales or to
secondhand stores. Many people sell their baby equipment as they
finish using it, so you can get fairly new items. Most good baby
equipment is made to withstand at least two rounds of children. If
your child is under two or three, you might want your family day
care mother to have a stroller. For one thing, you want to make it
possible for the kids to get to a park or playground regularly.

Day care centers and day care homes usually require you to
bring your own changes of clothing. Some centers keep track of the
number of diapers used and tack on a diaper charge to the weekly
fees. Numerous mothers tote their ubiquitous bag of baby things to
and from day care each day. But it will be much more convenient
to leave changes of clothing at the day care arrangement, taking
home dirty clothes and bringing new ones as necessary. You may
want to leave plastic bags (out of the children's reach) for storing
dirty clothes. Try leaving one change of clothes that matches the
current weather, one for cooler weather, one for warmer weather.
Some family day care mothers may be willing to wash any clothes
your child dirties along with her regular wash. This can be a real
convenience. (I have personally experienced finding spit-up-on
overalls — and worse — after they had been five days in a plastic
bag at the bottom of my baby tote bag.) Some day care centers

may have washers and dryers to handle bibs and blankets, and may do the children's dirty clothes as well.

Day care for the pre-potty-trained means disposable diapers. Most day care arrangements will not provide them. (Don't expect to find someone or someplace that will put up with cloth diapers. It's just too much to ask. I've met a few day care mothers who will deal with cloth diapers, but have never seen anything other than disposables at day care centers.) In some day care centers, you will see the state-of-the-art in diaper disposal and potty training: changing tables with high-power toilets built in for flushing away disposable diapers. Other centers have rows of small child-size toilets in their bathrooms. Perhaps this emphasis on waste disposal at day care centers derives from times when day care meant nursery, which meant hospital and sanitary.

In both family and center day care, meals and twice-daily snacks are usually provided. If the center does not have facilities to cook hot meals, then parents send a boxed lunch. Usually, kids receive a morning snack around 10:00 or 10:30, depending on how early most of them have arrived. The snack typically is juice or milk and cookies or crackers. Apple juice and graham crackers are always big favorites. Lunches are served early by adult standards: usually before noon. Naps routinely follow lunch. A second snack may be served after nap time or shortly before pick-up time, which begins about 4:00. The afternoon snack can be the same as the morning one, or a piece of fruit or something the children have helped make themselves.

Family day care homes tend to be less rigid about meal and snack times, feeding more on demand. Centers, because of their group size, tend to be more rigid and routinized about eating times. In centers, the play table usually doubles as an eating table. Therefore, eating times and play times must be kept separate if the caregivers are to avoid having Play-Doh eaten, and bread smashed into Play-Doh cans.

Infants are usually fed on demand rather than on a schedule no matter what type of care, and for obvious reasons. Centers and family day care homes usually expect that if your child isn't on solids yet, you will provide the particular brand of formula you like, or that you will leave frozen, expressed breast milk.

If your child has special dietary needs because of allergy, weight problems, religious reasons, or because you are vegetarian, macrobiotic, or an otherwise organic eater, you should be prepared to bring food yourself. It will be the responsibility of the caregiver to see that your child eats only what's on the diet. If your child has a serious disease that requires very strict dietary regulation (for example, diabetes), it will be best to avoid day care centers that have large numbers of staff, where the switching around of staff duties precludes a 100 percent guarantee that nothing forbidden is ever eaten. If you do send your own food, don't expect that doing so will significantly reduce the cost of day care. Little children just don't eat that much.

If your day care arrangement does provide food, you will be better off not bringing any supplements, especially treats. This sort of thing only causes hard feelings among the children.

If your day care center or family day care home requires you to bring food, you'll want to select foods that are easy to prepare ahead of time and that little children especially like. In addition, you may have to consider only those foods that can stand to be in a lunch box four or five hours without refrigeration. Here's a list of convenient foods from different food groups that your child may like (depending upon age).

- Eggs and Dairy Products
    Ready-mixed formula
    Yogurt
    Hard-boiled egg
    Cold scrambled egg
    Prepackaged small cheeses
    Macaroni and cheese
- Fruits and Vegetables
    Celery, carrot, cucumber, and even zucchini sticks
    Frozen corn or peas
    Peanut butter on anything
    Raisins in tiny boxes
    Other dried fruits/ fruit rolls
    Small cans of fruit juice
- Meats
    Baby meat sticks
    Vienna sausages

Bologna
Hot dog slices
Cold hamburger
Mini-raviolis
Spaghetti-o's
● Cereals and Grains
Little boxes of cereals
Granola
Trail mix
Graham crackers/ Ritz crackers
Arrowroot cookies/ Holland rusks (for teething)
Rice
● Treats
Small canned puddings
Cookies
Single serving potato chips
Halloween-size candy bars

There are also a number of convenient devices available that can make all the difference in putting together meals and snacks without a hassle: Flip and Sip thermoses with built-in straws in the lids, wide-mouth thermoses, zip and lock sandwich bags, a Tupperware lunch box with many containers that fit in it neatly, and Tupperware children's cups with two types of lids: one very tight-fitting with room for a small straw, the other a complete seal. Once you see how much easier such seemingly little conveniences can make preparing and transporting meals, you're bound to invent some more that suit your child's particular food likes and dislikes.

WHAT DO I DO WHEN MY CHILD IS SICK? _____

Some kids get sick more often than others. Some mothers worry about illness more than others. If you have a child who is often down with fevers, ear infections, sore throats, or diarrhea, it might really affect the type of care that you choose. Most day care arrangements frown on bringing sick children. It is unpleasant, at best, to conjure up the image of making 7:30 A.M. phone calls to friends to see who is willing to take care of the sick, screaming child you are holding in your other arm. A 1978 study found that the main reason women miss work is to stay home and take care of sick children.

If your child is being cared for at home, you will be unlikely to lose a day's work because of her illness. Your caregiver can just perform her duties as always. Your child will have all the possible comforts (except for you, of course).

Many family day care mothers are liberal about taking in sick children. It usually depends on how sick they are: runny nose, yes; coughing, yes; bad diarrhea, maybe not; fever, probably not. Each family day care mother seems to base her sick-care policies on how old the children she cares for are (the younger the kids, the stricter she'll be), how likely she feels she or her kids are to catch it, and how anxious she is about illness.

Day care centers usually have fairly strict rules about bringing in sick children. This is because of the monitoring that they are subject to by their state departments of public health. If a child becomes ill during the day, he will usually be isolated from the group (put on a cot in the director's office, perhaps). Some very large centers, much like elementary schools, have a nurse and/or an infirmary. In some areas of the country (for example, in Marin County, California, which has the highest rate of single-working-women heads of households per capita because of the divorce rate), there is a growing movement to establish special centers for sick children who would otherwise cause mothers to lose a day's work. These special sick centers would be community-run and open to children in all sorts of public and private day care in that city or town.

Many day care arrangements, especially centers, will require you to have alternative plans for when your child is sick. The idea is that it is better for one mother to spend two days at home, rather than for ten mothers to have to spend two days at home each, a week later, because their children all caught what the first one had. When this idea was first explained to me, it made good sense. But, as time went on, I noticed that most day care children, especially those in centers, seemed to have perpetual runny noses all winter long, nonetheless. This was true even in the centers that were very strict about not allowing children with symptoms. Too many children have runny noses too much of the time to continually be excluded from day care.

Naturally, you might assume that the more children grouped together, the greater the likelihood that illness would spread. There is contradictory evidence as to whether center day care children experience illness more frequently than family day care children or children at home. Children in family day care seem to have about the same risk of infection as children with families of the same size as the family day care group. Such findings, which are tied to group size, seem to say that the more children there are around, the greater the likelihood of infection. However, the research has not provided clear evidence that group size alone increases the risk of infection, but rather has shown that other factors are important too, including stability of the group. In other words, if the day-to-day composition of the group stays the same, there may be fewer risks for new infection. Day care children who are exposed to school-age siblings (or other school-age children, in the case of day care homes) may be more likely to get sick because school-age children are in contact with many potential carriers each day they are in school. Caregivers in centers who move from room-to-room (even though the kids stay in one place) may carry infection from one group to the next.

Children typically get about six colds per year. They may get a few more from their friends in day care, but we don't know whether this number is significantly more than they would have gotten at home. Children who are exposed to more children at day care than at home may not get any more colds than children from larger families.

Most frequently children carry bacteria that spread upper respiratory infections (URI) or viruses that cause diarrhea. Children who have already been exposed to the bacteria or virus may give the cold to another child without getting the cold themselves. One well child may infect another. Therefore, keeping children with symptoms of colds away from others is *not* a surefire way of preventing colds in other children in the day care arrangement.

Generally, the spread of minor childhood illnesses is not of concern by itself. Physicians are most concerned about the reoccurrence of minor illnesses in children who are also prone to other simultaneous infections, such as repeated otitis (ear infection), which theoretically could lead to hearing loss. It is not known whether recurrent minor childhood colds and illnesses lead to some degree of future immunity (say, by the grade-school years).

There are only a few childhood diseases (such as hepatitis or meningitis) that only on the rarest occasions have spread within a day care center. If one child does contract a serious disease, the center should have a policy of informing parents. Health care administered either by the center or a private pediatrician might include preventive prescription of a short antibiotic course to eradicate the condition in carriers and prevent its occurrence in other, healthy children.

Disease spread in day care can often be prevented or reduced. Diarrhea infections can be reduced by judicious handwashing between diaper changes and trips to the bathroom. Some centers recycle computer paper that they roll out on the changing table each time they change another child. Lacking paper, the changing areas and bathrooms should be wiped frequently with disinfectant. As for the actual mechanics of how diseases are spread, the nose is usually the culprit. Sneezing, therefore, as well as coughing and just breathing, are all means of releasing bacteria and viruses into the air. That's why it's more difficult to control the spread of URI than the spread of other minor childhood illnesses. The worst thing I've seen is caregivers who pick up one tissue and then go from kid to kid wiping noses but not changing tissues. (It's obvious what's wrong with that picture!) Young children may be especially susceptible to infections carried by older children. Keeping children out of mixed age groups and with children of their own age may help reduce the severity of colds. This theory is not proven, and it may be that age segregation is not a worthwhile preventive measure.

If you have any questions about day care and particular health problems that your child has had, consult your pediatrician.

WHAT WILL DAY CARE COST?

Working women often spend a shocking percentage of their take-home pay on child care. The preceding pages have enabled you to develop a picture of each type of day care more or less free of the pressure of how you might pay for it. When it comes to paying for day care, remember this first: *The worst day care is not always the cheapest, and the most expensive day care is not always the best.* How much convenience can you afford? This section outlines the relative costs of different types of care and how much you'll pay for care that is tailored to your lifestyle.

You will pay more for the care of younger children than older ones. A few major milestones in development are loosely related to points at which you can expect the cost of your day care to drop: crawling, self-feeding, walking, talking enough to make needs known, and potty-training. After potty-training the cost of day care levels off, until the time you begin to pay for a significant preschool component in your child's day. Preschool will cost more than center day care for children of the same age.

Care for two children will probably cost less than twice the amount paid for one. This is most usually true of in-home arrangements, sometimes also with family day care; least often the case for day care centers. (If you have more than two children of day care age and are working too, you well deserve any break on cost of care that you can find.)

Center day care is almost always the most expensive type of out-of-home care. Nationwide, the average cost (by average I mean the average of all states' reported medians) is $1.25 per hour for children under two. The state with the most expensive median cost of center day care for children under two is $2.44 per hour in Massachusetts; the lowest was $0.65 per hour in West Virginia. For center care children over two, the average cost, nationwide, was slightly less, $1.05 per hour. The most expensive center care for this age group was $1.70 per hour in Illinois; least expensive in Louisiana, $0.63 per hour.

The average national cost of family day care was $0.89 per hour. The highest cost was in Massachusetts ($1.50 per hour); the lowest, in Georgia ($0.50 per hour).

The average national cost of in-home care is difficult to specify. States seldom regulate in-home care, so the state agencies have no reliable way of knowing what it costs a parent. In fact, in-home care is probably the most expensive type of care. State agencies re-

Typical (Median) Cost of Day Care per Hour for Each Region of the U.S. for Each Type of Day Care

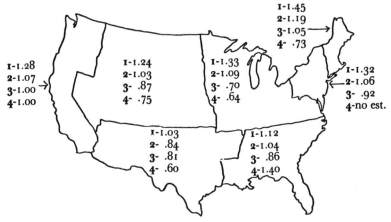

1- Center Day Care for Children Less Than Two Years Old
2- Center Day Care for Children Over Two Years Old
3- Family Day Care
4- In-Home Care

port that the cost of in-home care ranges from a minimum of $0.50 per hour (reported in Illinois) to a maximum payment at minimum wage level (paid in Oregon).

Personalized, in-home care can be quite expensive. You can expect to pay at least minimum wage (about $3.50 an hour) for someone to come to your home. If you expect to have housework done, as well as child care, you will pay more. But, interestingly, child care plus housework usually costs less than just housework. What does that say about our willingness as a society to pay good money for day care? What does that say about the value of children in today's society?

Often, in-home caregivers are relatives or friends of the family. This form of care tends to be inexpensive or free. Sometimes it's possible to barter your services in exchange for child care. For example, if your younger sister lives with you and cares for your little boy while you work, you could probably pay her $200 or so less per month than you'd normally pay a non–live-in caregiver, in exchange for her room and board.

If you currently use day care, or were expecting the worst in the way of cost, the figures quoted may seem optimistic. However, bear in mind that the agencies reporting these data have few or no records on the cost of private care; and the agencies largely base estimates of cost on the degree to which they will subsidize it. Since families who receive subsidies are poorer than most, these figures are probably a more accurate reflection of fees that lower income families rather than middle- or upper-middle-class families pay.

Since these estimates are, in all likelihood, as much as 50 percent lower than many of you are likely to spend, knowing the costs per se is not as valuable as knowing the relative expense of day care in your part of the country, compared to the nationwide averages. The map divides the United States into seven regions. It shows the average hourly cost of each type of day care for New England, the Northeast, the South, the East Central, the West Central, the Southwest, and the West Coast states. This map shows that day care costs are somewhat lower in the southern half of the United States than in the northern half. The two most northeasterly sections of the country tend to be most expensive.

Another factor that is partially visible on the map is that cost of day care is related to degree of urbanization. The cost of care in cities can be much higher than in suburban areas. A good illustration of this is in New York State, which subsidizes all kinds of day care at $1.37 per hour, except in New York City, where it will pay $1.94 per hour; about 30 percent more.

Subsidized Day Care

You don't have to have a very low income to qualify for a day care subsidy. There are many forms of subsidized child care. Sometimes employers chip in or run their own centers. Universities may run day care centers or day care homes with reduced fees for students. Most of the time, if you are eligible for a subsidy, you will be able to use it to purchase center day care or family day care. In these cases, the center care must be licensed, nonprofit, usually public; the family day care must be licensed or registered in accordance with state regulations. There are exceptions, especially if you receive a vendor-voucher or AFDC income-disregard form of subsidy, both of which will be described later in this section.

Most of the time, subsidies come from public money that filters down to people through state, county, city, or local nonprofit agencies administering funds to income-eligible families. There are several factors dictating who gets public money to help pay for their day care. In 1975, a piece of federal legislation called Title XX of the Social Security Act provided an amendment that gave block grants to social service agencies in each state so that they could help people pay for day care, among other things. In this case, a block grant meant that for every dollar the state put up, the federal government put up three. Then it was up to the state to apportion the money among various qualifying social services. Title XX provided the states with some contradictory guidelines, too. Theoretically, families who had incomes of less than 80 percent of the state median income (the median income is the most frequent, common, or typical income) were eligible for a full subsidy of their day care costs. That is, they could — but not necessarily would — receive a subsidy. It would depend upon how much money the state was willing to spend on child care. In addition, half of the openings at subsidized day care centers and in licensed day care homes were to be reserved for these eligible families.

It's useful to have a basic understanding of these regulations so you can see if you fit the criteria of income eligibility. However, even if you do, you may or may not be able to receive a subsidy. It will depend upon how many people in your state are worse off than you are and on whether they want child care subsidies, too. In order to make the system for meting out the money for day care subsidies fair, states sometimes add guidelines of their own that may (1) lower the percentage of median state income you need to earn in order to qualify, (2) specify a family size for a specific income level, (3) have a lower limit regardless of family size, or (4) use some combination of these. For example, in Connecticut, to qualify for day care subsidy, you need to earn less than 80 percent of the (1981) median state income of $18,000, which is $14,400 for a family of four. If you earn less than $7,500, you can get a full day care subsidy even if your family is just you and your child. In other states, even though the median income perhaps is higher, the percentage of median income may be lower. For example, in Arizona, a family of four must earn 60 percent of the state median income of $23,000 or less (that is, $13,800) to begin to qualify for a child care subsidy.

These examples give you an idea of how eligibility for subsidy is determined. As you can see, the requirements vary from state to state. In addition, these eligibility requirements are just the sort of thing state legislators like to play around with when they want to save some money. They may change unexpectedly and often. There are no hard, fast rules from state to state.

If you are eligible for a child care subsidy, you'll be interested in knowing exactly how this money is obtained. There are three main systems we'll discuss: sliding-scale payments; AFDC income disregard; and a new system, still on the drafting table in some states, the vendor-voucher system.

Sliding-scale payments are offered through publicly subsidized day care arrangements, centers, and sometimes family day care networks. Using criteria such as those I've outlined to determine whether a family of your size and income is eligible, the agency handling day care subsidies will offer to pay a certain portion of your child's fees on your behalf. Let's take the example of Connecticut again. If you earn $14,400 or less, you are theoretically entitled to *some* subsidy; if $7500 or less, a full subsidy. The average of those two amounts is about $11,000. If you earned $11,000, it would be reasonable for you to expect that charges of $2.00 per hour would "slide" down the "scale" of costs to $1.00 per hour; in other words, a 50 percent subsidy. The amount of subsidy — the amount you don't have to pay — will depend on funds available in the state for that purpose. In addition, many subsidies are preferentially awarded to families who have other needs besides financial ones. For example, single parents, welfare parents, and teenage parents, among others, are usually put at the top of the subsidy list.

For families with really low incomes, there is (among other things) the AFDC (Aid to Families with Dependent Children) income-disregard program. If you receive AFDC, this is one program designed to make it easier for you to "afford" to work. Before income disregard for child care expenses, if you earned only $600 per month, and spent $400 per month on day care for two children, you would have ended up with less money than if you stayed on welfare. With income disregard for child care expenses, if you pay some of your earnings for child care, you can "disregard," or deduct that amount when you figure your income for eligibility for AFDC. In other words, if you earn $600 per month, and pay $400 per month in child care, welfare will consider your income to be only $200 per month ($600 − $400 = $200) and reduce your AFDC payments minimally. The income-disregard program is particularly helpful to AFDC families who live in places where state-subsidized day care (for example, the sliding scale) is not readily available. Another nice thing about income disregard is that it can be used to pay for family day care or in-home care, as well as center day care.

A third type of subsidy is the vendor-voucher system. This is the newest of these types of programs. Some states have had it for a while, others are just starting up, still others don't use this alternative. Sometimes vendor-voucher programs exist under the more general title of "alternative payment programs." Vendor-voucher programs involve a "vendor," the seller of a child care service, such as a day care center or day care home; and the "voucher," the promise of payment to the vendor. Vendor-voucher programs take several forms and can be found in both public and private sectors of day care.

The agency that runs the vendor-voucher program (whether public or private nonprofit) usually gets money from a state agency to pay for day care for residents of a certain city or county. Most often the parent's voucher consists of reimbursement for all or part of already-paid child care bills, which are brought to the agency by the parent on a monthly basis. For example, in Oakland, California, there's a big day care referral agency called BANANAS. It gets money from the state that it can spend according to certain guidelines. Parents eligible for subsidy call for a referral and receive $2 for every $3 spent (66 percent subsidy) each month. Another example: the child care referral agency issues an I.O.U. for all or part of a child's day care fees. The parent can take this voucher (the I.O.U.) to a qualified center, which in turn submits it to the agency for payment.

A less typical version of a vendor-voucher program is when an employer offers to issue part- or full-payment vouchers as an employee job benefit. The employee can take her employer's voucher to the day care arrangement she chooses (the vendor) and use it to pay for day care. In the case of an employer-issued voucher, it is less expensive than maintaining and staffing a day care center for the children of employees. Vendor-voucher programs also give you, the income-eligible parents, more flexibility to choose day care that suits your needs, rather than being stuck with only those places that offer a sliding-scale method of payment.

The Child Care Tax Credit

No matter if you use in-home care, family day care, or a day care center, you will be able to claim a federal-income-tax child care credit on the money you spend. Some states also offer their own child care tax credit that works the same way as the federal credit. The state credit is usually a percentage of the federal credit. Among the states that now offer a child care tax credit on state income tax returns are Alaska, California, Colorado, Iowa, Oregon, and North Dakota. (Other states currently have child care tax-credit legislation pending, so check your state income tax forms to be sure.)

What is a tax credit? It's a lot better than a tax deduction! A tax credit is an amount you subtract from the amount of tax you would otherwise pay. If the amount of tax that you have already had withheld, plus the amount you owe, is still less than the amount of your child care tax credit, then you simply pay no tax, and get a refund for the withheld amount (but not for the child care tax credit amount that exceeds the amount of tax you would have otherwise paid). Don't worry, this will get clearer.

The child care tax credit was established as an economic incentive for families in which adults were not available to take care of children because both parents, or the single parent, was employed. The child care tax credit has been around for several years, but in 1982, a revised version was implemented for the first time. It's a bit more generous than the old credit and has been brought to us courtesy of Ronald Reagan's Economic Recovery Act of 1981. If you (and your spouse, if filing jointly) annually earn $10,000 gross adjusted income (wages, salaries, tips, dividends, interest, commissions) per year or less, you'll get the maximum child care tax credit available; with $30,000 gross family income per year or more, you'll get the minimum child care tax credit. The *maximum* credit is 30 percent of what you pay for child care, up to $2400 per year for your first child, $4800 per year for two or more children. The *minimum credit* is 20 percent of these same annual child care costs: $2400 for one child, $4800 for two or more. For those of you with incomes between $10,000 and $30,000 per year, you lose 1 percent of the 30 percent tax credit for every $2000 per year that you earn over $10,000 per year.

Dependent Care Tax Credit
by Family Income and Family Size

Family Income	Percent Credit	Maximum Amount of Tax Credit	
		1 CHILD	2 OR MORE
$10,000 per year or less	30	$720	$1440
$10,000–$11,999	30	$720	$1440
$12,000–$13,999	29	$696	$1392
$14,000–$15,999	28	$672	$1344
$16,000–$17,999	27	$648	$1296
$18,000–$19,999	26	$624	$1248
$20,000–$21,999	25	$600	$1200
$22,000–$23,999	24	$576	$1152
$24,000–$25,999	23	$552	$1104
$26,000–$27,999	22	$528	$1056
$28,000–$29,999	21	$504	$1008
$30,000 per year or more	20	$480	$ 960

An example: If your family earns $23,500 per year, you will be eligible for a 24 percent tax credit. Say you paid $60 per week for 50 weeks of the year ($3000) for child care for your one child. You get no credit on the last $600 you spent ($3000 − $2400 = $600). Twenty-four percent of $2400 is $576. You would subtract $576 *straight off the total tax* you would otherwise pay (or not have had refunded).

Another example: You jointly earn $45,000 and pay only $80

per week for a housekeeper to come in and watch your one- and two-and-a-half-year-olds, 48 weeks per year. That means child care costs you $3840 per year ($80 × 48 = $3840). This is $960 ($4800 − $3840 = $960) *less* than you could have received credit for spending. You are entitled to a credit of only 20 percent of $3840, which is $768. Again, $768 is subtracted from all the tax you owe.

If you and your spouse file separately, only one of you will be able to claim your child as a dependent. In many cases, it may be advantageous for the lower-earning spouse to declare your child as her/his dependent, because that spouse will have a lower income by which to calculate the percent of child care tax-credit eligibility. If you each earn more than $30,000 adjusted gross income, it won't make a difference on the child care tax credit whether you file jointly or singly.

Whenever you make child care payments (weekly or monthly), keep the stubs or canceled checks to substantiate your claim. If you don't use checks you'll need another type of receipt. The IRS recommends that you write on each check "Payment for Child Care." IRS form number 2441 must be filed with your return to get a "Credit for Child and Dependent Care."

Who's Eligible   The rules for whom the IRS considers an eligible worker; an eligible child/dependent; and an eligible caregiver, child care provider, or day care facility, are detailed in IRS form number 503, "Child and Disabled Dependent Care," but are summarized below.

An eligible worker has to be either a single head of household or second parent who is going to work. (In other words, there is no parent at home to care for the child.) You are considered an eligible worker if you are employed full or part time. If you work part time, you can claim a credit only for the part of the time you actually worked. Students are considered workers. Volunteers or those who receive a nominal salary (that is, below minimum wage) are not eligible workers. However, if volunteer work is required as part of an official educational course of study, you'll be entitled to a credit for child care while you do that work. You can also claim a child care tax credit for time that your child was in day care and you were looking for work.

An eligible child ("dependent," in the language of the IRS) is under fifteen years old, or is a disabled person of any age. A credit for full-time care is available only for children of preschool age (including kindergarten) or younger. First-graders up to fourteen-year-olds can only be claimed for after-school care. In addition, the child you claim has to be one of your personal exemptions on your own or joint income tax return.

Eligibility of caregivers and centers presents the most complex set of requirements. Let's take it one type of care at a time.

First, an in-home caregiver may be a housekeeper or other hired caregiver or a friend or relative. Any relative who is not your dependent will qualify, even if you live in the same house. Your own children who are under nineteen years old (or older, if a dependent student) are not eligible caregivers even if you pay them. If your child is nineteen or over and not claimed as a dependent on your tax return, you may pay her and claim a credit.

In some cases, an in-home caregiver, either live in or come in, will be a non-American citizen. If she is non-American she will need a work permit ("green card") and Social Security number so that you can report her earnings and get your credit. (Foreigners may apply for a Social Security card even though they are not allowed to work, because banks require a Social Security number to report to the IRS any dividends and interest that account holders earn.)

The IRS considers you the employer and your in-home caregiver your employee. You will need to contribute FICA and FUTA (Federal Unemployment Tax) for your caregiver, as well as withholding state and federal taxes from her income. (If you don't do these things and still try to take a child care tax credit, the IRS might get rather upset!!) If you dutifully pay FICA and FUTA, but don't report your caregiver's Social Security number, the Internal Revenue Service doesn't really seem to care. They only want the tax money and, if they get it, have no power to pursue matters with you any further.

To make the appropriate contributions at the correct times of the year, you'll need IRS form numbers 942, 940, W-2 (W-3 if you have more than one in-home caregiver that year), in addition to the regular IRS form number 2441 (the Dependent Care Tax

Credit) that everyone else uses. You'll also find it helpful to read IRS circular E to determine how much tax to withhold on your employee's behalf. You calculate the tax based on her projected annual salary. Withholding is due quarterly to the IRS. In addition to withholding tax on behalf of your in-home caregiver, you withhold half her FICA from her salary, currently 6.65 percent of gross income. Then, as the employer, you pay the other half of her FICA yourself, another 6.65 percent of her gross income. (These percentages are based on the 1981 tax year and may change.)

If you happen to take your caregiver off AFDC (welfare), or reduce her AFDC eligibility by giving her a job, you'll need IRS form number 906; you'll be eligible for the WIN tax credit instead of the regular child care tax credit.

If the worker is also a housekeeper, you must state to the IRS what percentage of her time is consumed by child care and what percentage is spent doing housework unrelated to the child. Payments for housework are not eligible for credit. The IRS expects you to make what they call a "reasonable allocation" when you subjectively decide what percentage of time was spent in child care and what percentage was not.

If you hire a caregiver through a domestic help or babysitting agency, the agency may be the employers rather than you. In that case, you pay the caregiver's salary to the employment agency, take a child care tax credit for that amount, and leave the IRS paperwork to the agency.

Claiming the child care tax credit is easier if you use family day care than if you have in-home care. A family day care mother is considered an independent operator of her own business and therefore is self-employed. You pay her an agreed-upon fee, and it's up to her to pay her own FICA and state and federal taxes. (You will still need her Social Security number, for identification only, on the IRS child care tax credit form.)

Regarding center day care, either a day care center or a nursery school is a tax-credit-eligible child care facility. As with family day care, you make all payments to the organization that runs the center and it deals with taxes.

If you receive a subsidy to help pay your child care expenses, you can claim a credit only for the balance you actually pay (after the subsidized amount has been subtracted from the fee). In other words, if the center's fees are $75 per week and you received a $25-per-week allowance in the form of a subsidy, discount, or scholarship (yes, some day care centers call it that), then you can only add $50 per week to the amount on which you will take a credit at the end of the year.

The tax credit is mainly meant to cover actual child care. However, an educational component or meals that are included as part of the center's fees are legal child care costs.

Incidentally, when you use family day care (or a day care center), the cost of transportation (by any means) to and from any day care arrangement cannot be claimed for credit.

If you have some special situation that doesn't seem to fit any of these general and peculiar rules, call your local office of the IRS.

Chapter 3

Determining Your Individual Child's Day Care Needs

FINDING THE DAY CARE that will be best for your child requires you to know what your child is like relative to other children his age, as well as what day care arrangements are available. When parents describe a day care arrangement and want to know whether it will be good for their child, there are several questions that I usually ask about the child's age, level of physical activity, verbal ability, dependency, reactions toward strangers, experiences with previous separations, and so on. Then I match the composite picture of the individual child's behavior and needs to the types of care that family has to choose from. This chapter will teach you to perform that process yourself.

Most research on day care, unfortunately, has not directly addressed questions that parents most often want answered. However, there is a sufficient body of accumulated information that logically allows us to infer many answers to questions about what type of day care is likely to be best for different children. Here are some of the questions that you probably have, and that this chapter will answer:

- How old should my child be when he starts day care?
- How physically developed does he have to be? Should he be weaned? Moving about: crawling, walking?
- Is it better to wait until he can talk?

- Will day care affect my baby's attachment to me?
- Will my child's temperament play a role in how he adjusts to day care?

This chapter deals with potential risk factors inherent in day care for children of different ages and levels of development. Much of the information is based on careful research. However, some areas of development that may be affected by attending day care have not yet been well researched. In those instances, we can weigh the pros and cons and speculate about possible effects. The younger a child, the more likely it is that day care will affect his development in some qualitative way. Potential risk factors are most relevant to children under three years old. But at any age, a child's personality and the type and quality of care he receives will interact in some unique way. If your child is less than a year old, please consider this information carefully. Much less is understood about the influences of day care on children less than a year old than on older children.

There are two ways to talk about how children differ from one another. There are developmental differences and there are individual differences. Each may influence your choice of day care arrangements.

The term developmental differences refers to stages or milestones of physical, social, and cognitive development. At each stage, children show increasing ability to do specific things. The term individual differences refers to the unique ways in which your child is different from other children of his age group. By studying the individual differences of children who are the same age, it's possible to understand the various ways a normal pattern of development can look.

Choosing child care based on your knowledge of your child's abilities and traits will be more important than considering his actual chronological age. Young children of the same chronological age vary a great deal in their stages of development.

A common misconception about child development is that the earlier a behavior (for example, walking or talking) develops, the "smarter" the child is or will be. In fact, earliness has seldom been shown to be related to adult competence. (Studies of brilliant mathematicians, such as Einstein, have shown that some geniuses consistently failed to talk until they were three years old or older.) In this chapter, you will be called upon to evaluate whether your child is "late" or "early" in some stage of development. Be frank with yourself. Remember that "late" or "early" doesn't really matter in the long run. What does matter is that you accurately assess your child's capabilities, and find for him a day care environment that suits his present needs.

What follows is a short course on a few basic concepts and methods that research psychologists use to describe aspects of development. Understanding these concepts should help you get a feeling for how researchers think about the effects of day care and just how much the research can and can't tell us.

Group Norm   In research that examines how children change as they get older, the findings are phrased in terms of how most of the children behaved. Results are couched in terms of means, averages, and normative behavior. Chances are that no single child in a study behaved exactly like the "average" child in every respect. Talking about the average or typical behavior is just a way of describing what is usually expected. A good deal of variation from the mean is normal and expected.

Stages   Many theories of development are based on the idea that learning occurs in stages. While there is some high-level theoretical-philosophical debate among child development muckety-mucks about the "reality" of stages, there is no doubt that the term is useful in describing behaviors that change rapidly from one form to the next, such as the various stages of a baby's motor development: rolling over is followed by creeping, then crawling, then cruising, then toddling, then walking, then running.

Critical Periods   Some theories include the idea that there are critical periods in development. During a critical period, a child experiences a heightened sensitivity to certain people, things, or events. As a result, events occurring during a critical period are expected to have a more lasting impact than events that do not occur during a critical period. An oft-cited example of a critical period is the imprinting period that immediately follows the birth of duck-lings. Konrad Lorenz showed that ducklings will imprint upon, or become attached to, whomever they see during this period, be it human or a mother duck. Research on day care has paid particular attention to possible critical periods in the formation of mother-in-fant attachment.

Inborn Characteristics   Another idea basic to some theories of in-dividual differences is that of inborn or innate characteristics. (Some psychologists specialize in debating whether such behaviors are genetically or environmentally determined.) No matter what you call it, exactly, these terms imply that from birth, or shortly thereafter, some component of an infant's personality is fixed. This fixed component may be small or large (depending on whom you believe or what component you are talking about), but always mixes with experience in order to be expressed in a unique way.

PHYSICAL DEVELOPMENT

There are several milestones in early physical development that are important to think of in terms of a day care arrangement.

As a general principle it's important to recognize that the greater a baby's physical autonomy, the greater his sense of psy-chological autonomy. Most babies who are less than six months old stay approximately where you put them. Between about six and eleven months, crawling begins. This lasts until cruising, when the baby maneuvers herself upright holding onto things. Between nine and fifteen months, walking usually starts.

These different means of self-propulsion are all important ways for babies to get to their caregivers when they need them. If your child is going to be in a day care arrangement with other children, it will be to her advantage to have some form of mobility.

On a more practical level, the middle of the first year is a time when progress in gross motor ability is rapid. Any day care ar-rangement you choose should be suitable or modifiable to accom-modate each of these stages. Just because your four-month-old doesn't go anywhere now, doesn't mean she won't be pulling the doilies out from under Grandma's teacups in another four months. If you choose an infant center or family day care home with only infants, be sure that there is enough space for the children as they get older.

Mobility, or the lack of it, is not one of the most critical factors to consider when deciding when to start day care. It's just one of a number of developmental building blocks to take into account.

Sleeping Schedule

Some mothers try to arrange day care around their child's sleep schedule. For example, a student mother may take her eighteen-month-old to day care in the morning so she can go to classes, then take him home for lunch and a nap, and do her homework from one to three in the afternoon while he sleeps.

But, nap times don't remain fixed. As a child grows up, he takes fewer naps and at different times of day than when he was younger. At birth, infants sleep or are sleepy between ten and fourteen hours per day. By six months, sleeping time may be down to two naps, say from 10:00 to 12:00 and from 2:00 to 5:00 each day, maybe less. By eighteen months, most children nap once a day, after lunch. Many give up naps altogether as they approach their third birthday, while others continue to take short late-afternoon naps into the primary school years. You may be one of the unfortunates, whose child stops napping before his second birthday.

Should children in part-time day care nap at day care or at home? I don't think it really matters, but you might consider not bringing your child to day care when he's asleep or sleepy. A child who's almost ready for a nap is likely to be cranky and fretful. It's a time when children feel very emotionally vulnerable. It's also a time when even minor irritations are perceived as monstrous distresses. When they're sleepy, children are more clingy and more reluctant to separate from their parents. A regular practice of bringing your child to day care when he's asleep might have a cumulatively stressful influence on him. Most children fight going to sleep because they are reluctant to leave their exciting world behind for a while. A child who associates sleep with the loss of his parent, even beyond the time of sleeping, might become very resistant to going to sleep at any time. Most children, though, will probably not be sensitive to this potential difficulty.

It can be very functional to arrange day care hours around nap time. You can minimize the number of hours that you are not available to your child. But since nap schedules evolve as the child matures, you should build flexibility into your day care arrangement to suit your child's future needs.

Feeding Times

Small babies, as you know, eat frequently. As they get older they eat fewer but more substantial meals, plus snacks. The need to eat while in day care becomes a psychological issue when nursing is involved. If you are going to nurse your baby while he's in day care, you'll need to be fairly close by and able to come and go easily. If you are nursing, you recognize the wonderful intimacy of feeding your baby yourself. Among other things, it signals your availability to the baby. It is an ingredient in building basic trust. But if your baby is going to be in day care, that trust will have to include others as well as yourself. Your baby will need to be able to take nourishment from others as well as from you (in both the physical and psychological sense). This is a very difficult issue for some new mothers because nursing is a symbol of the baby's exclusive and particular need of them. Nursing may be the aspect of parenting the baby that you are least willing to share — with the father, or with a caregiver. In a time of changing role definitions, nursing remains the only exclusively maternal privilege in child-rearing.

One mother I spoke with recently planned to begin leaving her three-and-a-half-month-old for the first time, full time, and continue a routine of 100 percent breast-feeding. She was to work about a mile from the day care mother and planned to nurse at drop-off time (about 9:00 A.M.), noon, and pick-up time (about 5:00 P.M.). As a nurse and wife of a pediatrician, she was well informed about the benefits of breast milk and didn't want the day care mother to give any supplements that might signal the beginning of the end for nursing. But anyone who's had a three-and-a-half-month-old knows how often they want to eat! Such a plan is unrealistic. If you're going to work, you just can't be a Superwoman on all fronts, even if you want to be. You can't selectively relinquish a part of child care without thinking about how your baby will react.

It's a very good idea, nutritionally, to try and sustain nursing through the first six months; one year is often recommended. But face it, if you are going to work or otherwise be away, and have a tiny baby too, you can't have everything. Any baby who is left for more than an hour needs to have recourse to something to eat. It's just unfair to the child any other way. The emotional comfort of receiving nutrition is indistinguishable from a sense of physical satiation of appetite for a young baby. Although your infant will not starve if he isn't fed for a few hours, he's likely to *want* to eat at some point. If he's fussy, he isn't happy. A caregiver who can't provide the baby what he wants will be bound to feel that she's doing an inadequate job and that her task is unpleasant. Don't put yourself, your caregiver, and especially your baby in that position. If you're going to use day care, leave expressed breast milk and/or formula with the caregiver. Arrange as many breast-feedings as you can, but leave the caregiver her own way of dealing with things as well.

As your child matures you will need to consider accommodating to his feeding schedule less and less. There may even be a point at which the benefits of breast-feeding are outweighed by the anxiety a mother's frequent coming and going from the day care arrangement may cause for an older infant of nine to twelve months old.

COGNITIVE DEVELOPMENT

Cognitive development refers to those aspects of the growing-up process that primarily involve thinking rather than physical or emotional development. Of course, these aspects of development are interwoven. Infants represent thought by action (for example, moving their mouths when they want to suck). Older children express emotions with words. Two rather different aspects of cognitive development, person permanence and language acquisition, will be discussed. These are perhaps the most important ones to consider when choosing day care.

Person Permanence

This strange-sounding descriptor comes from work based on the theories of Jean Piaget, the late eminent Swiss child psychologist, who created much of the vocabulary we now use to refer to phenomena of early cognitive development. What is known about person permanence suggests that you may want to wait until your infant can distinguish you as a parent before starting day care. That statement is not as simplistic as it sounds. Babies go through many stages of learning in order to differentiate parents from objects and from other people.

When an infant is born she sees objects in the same manner as you or I, but does not know where objects come from or where they go when they pass from sight. As time goes on, the infant recognizes some objects as things she's seen before. The most frequently appearing object is often the mother. The mother is also often the most salient, important object, since she is associated with the satisfaction of physical needs. Later the infant realizes that sometimes an object (or a person, such as the mother) is there, and sometimes it is not. As memory develops, the infant can remember and expect that an object will likely be where it was last seen. When the infant reaches the point where you can show her a toy, then cover it up, and she still knows it's under the cover (and not simply disappeared), she is considered to have achieved object permanence. Why is this important?

The development of person permanence is the same phenomenon, but involves the recognition and differentiation of people that the infant frequently sees. Person permanence develops in three main stages: at first (one to two months old), the parents' faces are not distinguished from those of other people. Second, the infant begins to show signs of recognizing the parents — quieting when held and smiling (one to four months old). Third, the infant develops the ability to remember where the mother is, even if she isn't directly visible. An infant's delight in reaching this third stage is demonstrated by the pleasure that he takes in playing peek-a-boo (five months old and older).

Attainment of person permanence means that the infant understands that the mother will return, once she leaves his view. There is a period, beginning after four to five months of age, in which the infant recognizes parents, but does not clearly differentiate whether they are out of sight, or out of the room, or out of the house.

No specific research has been done on whether it is better to begin day care during one stage of achieving person permanence than another. But one study showed that babies who develop object permanence before person permanence (perhaps because there is not enough consistency in the appearance of one adult) were more likely to be insecurely attached to the mother at one year of age. It's possible to make some educated guesses. In terms of cognitive development, your child should be developed enough to clearly recognize you, apart from other individuals, before you leave her (two to four months). It might be even better to wait until your child has attained person permanence. After achieving this stage, things reach a plateau for a while. Only a much older infant or toddler (perhaps fourteen months to two years old or older), who can understand some language, can take solace in verbal reassurances that you will return.

Language Acquisition: Day Care as a Place to Learn to Talk

Learning to talk is a fundamental feature of cognition. When thinking about day care, it is important to consider what type of environment might be most beneficial to the growth of language, and what kind of language stimulation children of different ages need most when in day care.

Language acquisition is a natural by-product of early "turn-taking" between parent and child:

> Father tickles infant. Infant coos.
> FATHER: Oh, you want me to tickle more?
> INFANT: *waves arms*

FATHER: Yes, oh, you're ticklish!
INFANT: *burps*
FATHER: Oh, you funny baby!

And so on.

Each action of the infant, no matter how involuntary, is taken by the father as a response to his actions and words. Using this type of give and take as a prototype, linguists and psychologists have built two basically different theories about how language develops.

The first is a behaviorist theory as explained by B. F. Skinner and others who believe that language is learned through a trial-and-error process. Children are praised (positive reinforcement) for appropriately imitated language, and ignored, misunderstood, or corrected (negative reinforcement) for inappropriate language use. Behaviorist theory suggests that having an adult who constantly models and corrects language is a necessary condition for learning to talk. Behaviorists, then, would feel that a day care arrangement where the child is listened to and is spoken to directly and frequently would be very important if that child is going to learn to talk. Behaviorists would say that being addressed as part of a large group of children would not be as likely as individualized care to give a child an opportunity to respond and thus be reinforced. A behaviorist would probably recommend one-to-one or small-group care for the child who's just learning to talk.

On the other hand, there is the nativist theory of language development as explained by Noam Chomsky and others. To capsulize, nativists believe that humans alone have an innate ability and drive to learn rules of language. Some nativists suggest that the child does this by playing the role of "mini-linguist," observing adult speech, making hypotheses about language structure and use, testing hypotheses, revising them, and then testing them again. Nativists see this rule-making process at work in the way that children overgeneralize a rule of grammar (for example, *s* plurals: correctly saying "shirt-shirts," "shoe-shoes," but "shorts-shortses"). Children often fail to comprehend exceptions to grammatical rules. Since nativists believe that language comes from observing others speak, they might be less inclined than behaviorists to say that one-to-one or small-group settings in day care are necessary when learning to talk. Instead, a nativist might put his child in a day care center with lots of group story time, TV, and records, but less emphasis on direct caregiver-child conversation.

Who is right? The behaviorists or the nativists? From some studies that have been done, the answer appears to lie between these extreme views.

First, there is evidence that motherese, a mother's use of baby talk, promotes language learning. Motherese is special speech to young children in which sentences and words are kept short; simple grammar is used; the frame of reference is the present tense; intonation is exaggerated; and words or phrases are often repeated. Motherese provides both the modeling that behaviorists say is important and the grammatical clarity that nativists say is important.

There is further evidence that children need individualized, one-to-one language experiences. Two researchers reported on the intriguing case of a normal, hearing child of deaf parents who had largely failed to learn to speak, even though his parents turned on TV and radio for him. (Later, after speech therapy, his language became normal.) Other researchers have noted that children will not learn a foreign language through TV alone.

Hearing language is not enough. Children must be spoken to, and in a way they understand. But do only mothers (and other adult caregivers) use motherese? No. Another study showed that children as young as four years old will adjust their language and attempt to use motherese for two-year-olds! Therefore, young children in day care (at least in mixed age groups) will be helped in learning to speak by slightly older children.

Day Care and the Child's Ability to Communicate

Very young children can, of course, make their wants known, long before they can talk. The first stage of language development is prereceptive. Until about nine to twelve months of age, children do not demonstrate that they comprehend (receive) the actual meaning of most of what is said to them. Instead they respond primarily to the tone of voice you use and a few key words such as

No!! Receptive language comes next. This is still a preverbal phase of language development, in which the child can act upon "Bring the ball to Mama!" but cannot speak and say "OK, I'm bringing it!" The third phase of language development is productive or expressive language, when the child says (produces) words.

Within each of these phases we can examine both the child's linguistic competence and the child's communicative competence. Linguistic competence refers to the ability to use spoken language effectively. Communicative competence refers to the ability to convey meaning in many ways: through words, as well as nonverbally, taking advantage of context, tone, crying, smiling, laughing, pointing, and grunting. When a child does not yet speak, actual linguistic competence is not as important a factor as communicative competence. Some preverbal children are more communicatively competent or advanced than others; that is, they are better at letting you know what they want.

How does this affect which type of day care you will choose? Overall, preverbal children are dependent on communicative competency — an ability to make themselves understood even though use of words is minimal or nonexistent. Such a method of communicating is highly individualistic, consisting of signals and abbreviated words and baby talk referring to things in the child's own personal realm of experience. Preverbal children need a day care arrangement in which the caregiver can spend enough individual time with each child to know the meaning of each child's particular signals. For example, a good caregiver knows that thirteen-month-olds have any number of ways of signaling a dirty diaper: they might squat, sit in one place, walk with a wider gait (or do nothing at all). A child who has a reliable set of these signals is more easily understood than a child who does not always use the same signals for the same things. Some fussy children will give the same whine whether they want a toy, want to eat, or want to be changed.

For example, I observed a fifteen-month-old boy as he watched his day care mother stir a half-gallon jar of old-fashioned peanut butter. He kept shaking his head no, and looked rather upset. What did this nonverbal behavior mean? His astute day care mother finally asked, "Do you think this is dirty diapers, Sammy?"

Sammy nodded his head yes. The day care mother knew the face this child used when his diapers were dirty.

How easily do you pick up these kinds of cues from your child? Ease of understanding, of course, increases with the child's age. The point is, if your child's needs are difficult to determine, you will have more reason to choose an individualized form of care. Children who make their needs known clearly and easily are more likely to be content and adapt well in larger groups since caregivers can easily satisfy their needs.

As a rough rule of thumb, children who do not yet speak need one primary caregiver: in-home care or family day care. After your child can use basic words, he will be better able to make his wants clear in a way that everyone understands. That caregiver should be an adult who can speak directly to him in a way that is neither too hard and incomprehensible, nor too babyish and unchallenging for his individual level of development.

DAY CARE AND ATTACHMENT

There are three questions about attachment parents who are putting their children into a day care arrangement most often ask:

1. Will day care change my child's attachment to me?
2. Do children with different types of attachments to parents adjust differently to day care?
3. How long do I have to wait until my child's attachment to me is developed enough to start a day care arrangement?

To answer these questions, it's first necessary to define *attachment.* Attachment is a process in an infant's social development by which he comes to love, trust, and rely upon one or more primary caregivers. Most children have one person to whom they are most strongly attached, most often their mothers. Fathers are usually a close second. Attachment theorists used to favor the idea that children could have only one real, secure, close primary attachment. A ground-breaking Scottish study published in 1964 showed that by eighteen months old, infants typically had about three attachment figures. Therefore, it is reasonable to assume that children in day care may become attached to both parents *and* caregivers.

Attachment is sometimes referred to as bonding. Pediatricians and natural childbirth practitioners tend to use this term. *Bonding* derives from animal ethology research, while *attachment* is more often used to describe humans. I prefer the term attachment because it makes me think of human babies and not rat pups.

Psychologists originally became interested in the effects of day care on attachment because earlier work on maternal deprivation had shown that permanent loss of the mother could produce devastating effects on institutionalized infants. These studies of marasmus and hospitalism were mentioned in chapter one. John Bowlby's 1951 World Health Organization monograph entitled "Maternal Care and Mental Health" made known the findings of these maternal-deprivation studies and played a crucial role in mobilizing subsequent research on mothering in general, and day care in particular.

Later, other researchers found negative effects of several weeks' separations, much like those seen in the institutionalized children. These negative effects included withdrawal from social contact and depression while the parents were away; and when parents returned, the children either avoided the parents or clung to them. These behaviors are all extreme signs of disturbed, anxious, insecure attachments. Later, these children reestablished rapport with their parents, but the researchers believed that under stress, these children would regress to their old, insecure ways.

Much of the stress that the child undergoes when separated from a parent involves getting used to the fact that the parent is not there. As day care became more widely used, psychologists began to wonder whether coping with frequent, daily separations might cause a child to develop an insecure attachment to his mother. It was suspected that both the repeated and cumulative impact of frequent separation might build up more anxiety than a young child could cope with successfully.

To date, a large number of studies have assessed the effects of day care on mother-child attachment. There has been disagreement among researchers about the absolute accuracy of the methods of some of these studies, but the findings have nonetheless been remarkably consistent in showing no direct, main effect of day care on previously secure mother-child attachments in most children. Research has pretty much given day care a clean bill of health as far as effects on mother-child attachment go. But the intricacies of these studies have brought to light some other possible sources of concern. I think that most day care researchers aren't 100 percent certain that some future study won't show that day care, along with some other intervening factor, such as temperament, or prior insecure attachment to parents, is related to ill effects on the child.

Accurately measuring children's actions and reactions in day care is very tricky business. It is likely that the kinds of measures used may not be the right ones to determine if day care has negative effects on later development.

For example, one of the earliest studies of day care and attachment found that day care did make children insecurely attached. However, that study has been largely discredited, because the researcher neglected to determine whether the children she studied had been insecurely attached before starting day care.

Other, later studies were more carefully done and found few or no ill effects of day care on attachment. These studies have typically examined children between the ages of three and one-half months and four years old, including children in high- and low-quality care, from middle-class as well as poor families. Although most children seem to remain securely attached to their mothers even when they attend day care, these studies do point to some possible exceptions or "risk factors": children from unstable families (moving, divorcing, et cetera) may have a harder time in day care. Children who attend day care for many hours rather than fewer hours may have a harder time. Younger children are more stressed than older ones. Children in ultra-high-quality day care are probably less at risk than children in less well-regulated and more questionable-quality care. Also, some children are going to be securely or insecurely attached for any number of reasons, whether or not they ever attend day care. That's just how some children are.

Security of attachment is determined by some processes that are understood, as well as by some factors that remain unexplained. Probably, strength of attachment is determined in part by the parents' behavior and partially by the innate character of the child. Parents who treat each of their children quite similarly may have some children who behave securely attached and other children who behave less securely attached.

The question that research has not really addressed is: do insecurely attached children adjust to day care differently than securely attached children? To answer this question it's necessary to review how it's possible to judge whether a child is securely attached to the parent. You can try to determine whether your child's own attachment behaviors seem to be more typical of one type of attachment than others.

When psychologists classify a child's attachment to the mother they often do so by recording the child's behavior during a rigidly prescribed series of laboratory episodes called the Strange Situation. The child is in a room with the mother and a female stranger who alternately play with him, and enter and leave the room. The Strange Situation suggests a few key behaviors that are related to a child's quality of attachment to parents. Although the Strange Situation most often involves a mother and child, it is an analog for the child's relation to either parent, in or out of laboratory conditions.

Showing distress on separation and relief or happiness upon reunion, and using the parent as a base from which to explore are signs of secure attachment. In the Strange Situation, secure children frequently approach or talk to their mothers as a means of reassurance that the mother is still available. As children get older and less dependent upon the mother, this sort of behavior becomes less pronounced. Three- and four-year-olds do these things much less than one- or two-year-olds.

Children who are described as insecurely attached have two main ways of expressing themselves to their parents. Some avoid the parents when they return after having been away for even a brief time. Some insecurely attached children will avoid their mothers after simply having been left alone in a room, which is what happens in the Strange Situation. Some children who avoid their parents may be doing so because they are angry at having been left. Some psychologists disagree with this interpretation and believe that parental "avoidance" sometimes occurs when the child is really very engrossed in play, and is unaware of the parent's return. Another, more problematic explanation of avoidant behavior in children who have attended day care is that they really aren't insecurely attached at all; they are just used to having their parents come and go.

Other insecurely attached children may resist a parent's attempts to greet them or be affectionate. These children may initially greet a parent, only to push away when picked up and hugged. At other times, these children tend to be more clingy and reluctant to explore when in an unfamiliar place. Sometimes this resistance is described as a resistant ambivalent attachment to the mother: the child experiences feelings of both love and anger toward the parents.

There is little research to help understand whether children with different initial attachments may adjust differently to day care. The research does suggest that most securely attached children as well as avoidant (insecure) children adapt well to day care. In one Stanford University study of temperament and mother-child attachment, some of the children studied happened to have attended day care, while others had not. Although the primary purpose of this particular study was not to look for day care differences, the researcher was impressed that avoidant children appeared more independent than others when playing in a novel situation. This tentatively indicates that children who appear to be somewhat avoidant might actually be quite positively independent. The mothers of these children describe them that way. Further, avoidant patterns might really help a child cope with the strangeness of a new day care arrangement. Such children may be less bothered by their mother's absence since they tend to focus on things other than their mother when they are in a new place. However, it is still not known whether children who use avoidance as a coping strategy are as well off as children who seem to be more securely attached.

How Attached Do Children Have to Be Before Starting Day Care?

A review of the stages of attachment may be used to identify points in development that seem to be better than others for starting day care for the first time. Infants first begin to differentiate familiar and unfamiliar faces at about one to four months of age. A young infant may be distressed when a familiar face leaves, but typically quiets quickly. Older infants tend not to quiet until the familiar person returns. At this point infants can distinguish parents from strangers but don't show real aversions to strangers as they do later on. Most infants who go through fear of strangers have reached this stage by six to ten months of age. For mothers who plan an early return to work, it is advisable to do it sometime between the time your child recognizes you (one to three months) and before your child begins to be apprehensive of strangers (six to ten months). Even if you are not quite ready to start leaving your child on a regular basis, a part-time arrangement during this "window" might get your child used to having you come and go.

The hallmark of the fear-of-strangers phase is the babe-in-arms who cuddles face-in to the mother's shoulder as soon as an unfamiliar adult smiles or says hello. Typically, this is a passing stage, which grows less intense as the infant becomes older and more interested in the world away from Mama, declining between fourteen and twenty months of age. Some children never do become fearful of strangers. It makes sense that if your child is really going through stranger anxiety, it is probably not the best time to start day care.

If you begin to leave your child with unfamiliar caregivers at this point, you may only be confirming your baby's unvoicable suspicions that her primary attachment figure's availability cannot be assured. You may be unnecessarily protracting and overemphasizing the difficulties of a fairly transitory period in development.

If you must return to work at this point, provide your child with extra opportunities to become familiar with new caregivers and the new environment before leaving. You could help bridge the gap of unfamiliarity in the day care setting by staying with the caregiver for a couple of days, returning after only brief exits, or bringing familiar toys and a blanket to the new setting.

Rather unfortunately, many mothers plan to return to work at the time of their child's first birthday. While the one-year benchmark is certainly a time to look back on the previous year's accomplishments, it is seldom the optimal time to start day care. It is usually at the peak of stranger anxiety. A good time to start day care may be at the point when the infant's very active seeking of the mother's physical presence begins to decline after fourteen to twenty months old. You should take your cues about activeness of attachment from your child's behavior, and not from his chronological age. For example, an early walker may start stranger anxiety at six months, and be coming out of it by nine months. Such a child might easily start day care at ten months. Another ten-month-old, who does not yet walk, may have only recently started to scream with fear each time she is left alone in her room for even a second. Once a child has physical mobility, she begins to develop a greater sense of control over her environment and these reactions tend to begin diminishing.

DAY CARE AND TEMPERAMENT

Will the temperament of your child have anything to do with the way he takes to being in day care? It may. There is presently no completed research on how temperament may play a role in a child's adjustment to day care. Day care researchers are becoming more convinced that temperament may be one key factor in adjustment to day care.

Temperament is one way of describing a child's personality. A group of temperamental characteristics together is often referred to as a behavioral style. Much of the major research on temperament was initiated by Stella Chess, Alexander Thomas, and their colleagues at the New York Longitudinal Study (NYLS). These researchers have described nine different aspects of temperament, each one present in every child to some degree. Here's a brief quiz on your child's temperament. As you read, record the descriptions that best apply to your child.

1. Q: What is your child's level of physical activity?
   A: *high   medium   low*

2. Q: How predictable are your child's physical needs, such as hunger and sleep?
   A: *regular   variable   irregular*

3. Q: Is your child wary or exploratory when faced with new things and/or a new environment?
   A: *more likely to approach   variable   more likely to withdraw*

4. Q: How easily does your child accept new things after a trial period (as differentiated from initial "approach" to new things)?
   A: *adaptable   variable   nonadaptive*

5. Q: How much stimulation does it take to get your child excited?
   A: *much   medium   little*

6. Q. How intensely does your child react to things around him?
   A: *high energy   variable   low energy, mellow*

7. Q: What kind of a mood is your child in most of the time?
   A: *positive (happier than most)   variable   negative (unhappy more than most)*

8. Q: Is your child more easily distracted than most?
   A: *yes (easily)   variable   no (not easily)*

9. Q: Is your child able to maintain interest in one thing for a long time?
   A: *yes (long attention span)   variable   no (short attention span)*

As you've read through these descriptions of different aspects of temperament and tried to evaluate your child, you've probably noticed at least two things: first that your child scored in the middle many times; and second, that many aspects of temperament seem to overlap, and therefore if your child is high on one, it will almost certainly follow that your child will be high on the other.

Based on a rating of different aspects of temperament, many children can be described as having one of three *behavioral styles* (about 35 percent of children don't fit one style perfectly, but fall somewhere in between them):

1. Easy: about 40 percent of all children can be described as easy, with regular physical needs, adaptable to new things, positive in new situations, having a positive mood much of the time, and using moderate emotional intensity in their reactions and interactions. (Your child probably fits this description if you scored him difficult no more than twice; easy most of the rest of the time.)
2. Difficult: about 10 percent of all children can be described as having irregular patterns, respond negatively to new things, cry frequently, are easily frustrated, and often are intensely negative. (Your child probably fits this description if you scored him as difficult four or five times or more.)
3. Slow to warm: about 15 percent of all children can be described as slow to warm; in other words, they are mildly negative to new things but adapt positively after an initial adjustment period. On other dimensions of temperament, these children sometimes behave like easy children, at other times like difficult children. (Your child probably fits this description if you scored him as showing "withdrawal" on number 3, and "nonadaptive" on number 4, almost regardless of moodiness or overall activity level.)

All of these types of children are normal. The differences between these groups are all within normal range. But these children perhaps can be expected to differ in the way in which they adjust to day care.

Often, difficult children have the hardest time in day care. They tend to be very active and difficult for caregivers to control and to relate to personally. It's often hard to know what these children want when they want something. Often day care centers are best for difficult children who are very active because centers usually provide more opportunities for a physical workout than home-based care. In centers they get less negative feedback from adults who become frustrated at controlling them. The environment is child-centered, so *no* is not the only word the difficult child hears. The more fixed routines at centers allow difficult children to learn to adapt — eventually. Routines can be particularly helpful for children who have problems regulating themselves.

Slow-to-warm children can be expected to have initial adjustments problems, suggesting a more gradual increasing of the hours in day care before entering full time care. Since the slow-to-warm child's main problem lies in making initial adjustment to new situations, you might expect that after some difficulties early on, long-term adjustment would be just fine. If you recognize your child to be slow-to-warm, you should make special efforts to allow a gradual adjustment to day care, setting things at the child's pace. It may also be that slow-to-warm children are those who experience the most prolonged or intense stranger anxiety during development of attachment. If this seems to be the case with your child, I would especially recommend waiting to start day care until fear of strangers is on the decline. Slow-to-warm and resistantly attached children share many of the same hesitations about new things. Often, resistant children seem to be describable as slow-to-warm and vice versa.

An easy child would be the most certain to take well to day care from the beginning and to acclimate well to his new surroundings. An easy child is one who might never go through the phase of stranger anxiety at all. The age you pick for starting an easy child in day care will probably not be as crucial as for a child with a less receptive behavioral style.

COGNITIVE STYLE

A child's cognitive style may similarly influence the way in which he adjusts to a new situation such as day care. Cognitive style refers to the way in which children go about getting and using information. In young children, cognitive style would refer to the way children go about their perpetual exploration of where they are. For example, some children are more oriented toward toys. Others are more oriented toward people. Some children feel satisfied by their own activity, while others derive more satisfaction from being praised by adults.

The aspect of cognitive style that may be most related to day care adjustment is the child's degree of "field independence" versus "field dependence" or "field sensitivity." One study showed that children who were field-independent worked well independently, were competitive, valued individual recognition, were task-oriented, like to try new things, but were not very inclined to want physical contact with the teacher. Children who were field-sensitive liked working cooperatively, were more likely to pay attention to the opinions and feelings of others, were more dependent upon personal praise, and related more directly and less formally to the teacher than did field-independent children. Teachers got along best with children who reflected their own cognitive style.

Studies of "locus of control" have addressed similar concerns about children's means of coping with their environments. Children who can be described as having an internal locus of control are rather field-independent. More field-dependent children can be described as having an external locus of control.

This research suggests that children who externalize may do better in day care arrangements where there's lots of opportunity for personal, one-to-one contact with the caregiver. More internalized children, on the other hand, seem to be better off if the caregiver isn't on top of them, such as in a group care setting.

PUTTING IT ALL TOGETHER: WHICH DAY CARE FOR WHICH CHILDREN?

Ideally, a picture of your child relative to others has emerged from this mélange of jargon and new ideas. You've had an opportunity to assess how grown up your child is, compared to other children of the same age, as well as how your child is different as an individual from others of the same age.

It is so very difficult to recommend day care without the opportunity to know an individual child. What follows are my personal guidelines based on knowledge of developmental and individual differences.

I think that in-home care is best for young babies. Such an arrangement may be ideal throughout the first year. It will provide your child with all the familiarity of home, and the benefits of individualized care. The earlier in the first year that you start care, the more important it will be to have it in your own home. By the third and fourth quarters of the first year, its importance lessens.

I think that family day care is ideal for one- and two-year-olds. There is exposure to peers, but also a homelike environment and one significant adult. All the prerequisites for development that call for one-to-one communication with a primary caregiver are present in a context that can still be varied and stimulating because of many toys and other children. More difficult, less secure, and less communicative children will benefit from family day care for a longer period of time, because it has the potential to be flexibly responsive to that kind of child's special needs. By the time a child can speak well, the need for family day care lessens.

I think that center day care is most appropriate for children two and one-half years old (i.e., good speakers) and older. Very secure, easy, independent, or very physically active children may be ready for a center sooner. The center provides less individualized care, more challenges to be independent. The child needs to be able to be more dependent upon his own resources, rather than upon any adult's. Since centers can offer more stable care over a period of years than other, less formal arrangements, they may be most important for children who are experiencing many changes in other aspects of their lives.

These statements do not mean that no infant should be in a center, or that no four-year-old can do well with a caregiver in his own home. It depends on the child. It depends on the care arrangement. And it depends on you, the parent.

Chapter 4

Locating Child Care Arrangements from Which to Choose

YOU'RE READY TO GO out and locate some potential day care arrangements. Options are essential! You really *must* consider a variety of arrangements before making a decision. This message will be repeated in different ways throughout this chapter because it's so very vital. Almost all day care arrangements that go bad quickly do so, at least in part, because the parents did not look at a number of arrangements before making a decision. The parents did not stop and take a hard look and think, "What could be better?" In this chapter, we'll talk about *where* to look. Then, in the next chapter, we'll talk about *how* to look.

I have never ceased to be amazed at how little time many parents spend looking for day care. For a long time, I just couldn't figure out why parents don't look around more than they do. Some, unfortunately, just don't know how to look or where to look. Others allow their perceptions of their lives as just not "together" enough to excuse them from putting more time into a task that might really have important implications for their child's development. But beyond that, there is a very basic, deep-seated reason that parents do not check out more day care alternatives: it is emotionally draining. Just thinking about starting your child in a day care arrangement can seem like a huge hurdle. To make things worse, most children start day care as their mothers return to work. The mother has her new job responsibilities to worry about. The father usually has to expend energy acclimating to changes in his role in the household and in his outside commitments as well. Parents, like all other healthy people, want to spend as little time as possible inflicting somewhat painful experiences upon themselves.

One rationalization that parents frequently use is to think of why a particular day care arrangement will be good, while not spending equal time thinking why it could be bad. This leads to some strange stories. One father told me, "When we found this Brazilian woman, we thought, Wouldn't it be great for Aaron [aged two weeks] to learn to speak Portuguese? Even though I can't speak Portuguese ... I can learn. ..." The parents were not primarily concerned with the fact that their ability to communicate with the caregiver (who did not speak English) was going to be quite limited.

Each time parents conjure up a mental image of a possible day care arrangement, they see their child in that strange new place, with strange people, doing things the parents will never see. This is disquieting, and also definitely part of the process of choosing day care. It has to be acknowledged, and overcome. Ignoring or diverting the discomfort of this mental image may be a successful stopgap measure, but in no way will it do anything good for your children (or for you in the long run). Parents' feelings of apprehension are real. Examine them. You should use them to motivate yourself to find good day care. Putting those feelings away cheats yourself and your child.

A case in point: one day I ran into a social-worker with whom I had earlier discussed her intention to change her two-year-old's day care arrangement (he was in an excellent infant center). I asked her if she had made any progress. Looking slightly embarrassed, she said, "Not yet. ... I've been so busy with my work. ..." Then she observed, "Isn't it strange that I spend all day helping other people's kids, but have put this important issue concerning my own kid to the back of my mind?" I agreed; it's strange, but very much what parents do when confronted with difficult choices regarding their children.

I am always concerned when I find out that otherwise rational, even overprotective parents have checked out only one or two day care alternatives. I don't think anyone can really know what they want in a day care arrangement until they see what's available.

Some parents deal with the arduous issue of choosing day care by throwing money at it. (The theory is that the more something costs, the better it is. While this theory may work for designer clothes and oriental carpets, it is seldom true of human services.) The quality of day care is all too often equated with cost. Day care centers and day care mothers who claim to charge more because they provide "exceptional" quality almost always get the fees they demand. But more often than not, the quality that is being offered can be purchased elsewhere at the going rate. The point is, you shouldn't use your ability to pay more than average for day care as a substitute for spending time conducting a thorough search for possible child care alternatives.

Being a consumer of day care services is just like being the consumer of any other costly product. No one would buy a TV, car, or house without turning on a number of TVs, driving a few cars, or looking at the other houses in the neighborhood. It is *at least* this important to be a discriminating consumer of child care. You can get new TVs, cars, and houses if you happen to buy a lemon. A child is a priceless commodity. You are "buying" something that will influence your child's development.

Day care is a major expenditure at a point in family-life development when most families don't have a lot of money to spend. Consider this. If your child is in full-time care from age one until age five when she starts kindergarten, that's four years of day care. Let's try a fairly modest $50 per week for fifty weeks a year, or $2,500 per year. That's at least $10,000 you'll spend by the time your child's ready for kindergarten. Five years of day care at $80 is twice that. Chances are, if you're thirty years old or older, your college education didn't cost that much! Back to the car-buying analogy: would you buy the first $10,000 car you saw, let alone drove?

WHEN TO START LOOKING FOR DAY CARE

How far ahead must you plan for day care? There are two things to consider. First, how old your child will be when she starts day care; and second, how available the type of care you want is for a child of that age. More advance planning will be needed when waiting lists are involved. Waiting lists are usually longer for younger children (less than two years) than for older ones (over two years). If you want out-of-home care at the same place for two or more of your children together, you can add to your advance-planning time.

If you anticipate that your child may need a couple of weeks to ease into day care, you'll need to plan for two start dates, a week or two apart. The first start day will be when you leave your child the first time, and the second will be after you've gradually incorporated the number of hours you need to be away; that is, the date you actually start or return to your job.

If you are going to use center day care, the overall number of center day care slots in your community and the waiting lists for them will be your nemesis. If you're going to be eligible for a subsidy, you can add anywhere from a month to six months to your advance-planning time because of the limited number of publicly subsidized day care slots. However, sometimes being income-eligible for subsidy, or being a single parent, or other factors, can help you go to the top of the waiting list (or at least ahead of other, higher-earning families). While this is nice for the subsidized families, I often side with more middle-class mothers who stay on waiting lists for months, prepared to pay their own money for child care, while subsidized families take "their" slots and make the middle class "pay" for it (with their tax money) to boot. (This is one of many day care policy issues that still needs to be equitably resolved.)

The time of year is another factor in when to start to look for day care. September and then January are the busiest times for starting new day care arrangements. Allow an extra couple of weeks or so for your search around these months.

Day care centers often have waiting lists. (I've never seen an already-established center worth its salt that didn't have a waiting list for full-time slots.) New centers are more likely to have openings than established ones. Day care centers run for members of a limited group, such as those sponsored by colleges, tend to be overutilized and to have very long lists. Once, I was going through the waiting list of one of the Stanford University day care centers to locate subjects for research. In the place where the parent was supposed to fill in "name of child," it said "No name/seven months pregnant." This woman wanted day care for when her yet-to-be-born child would be six months old! This was the first time, though not the last, I'd heard of such a thing. It may be difficult for some prospective parents to be quite that calculating. However, there are times when that sort of advance planning is exactly what is needed.

Center care is *least* available for children under two years old, comprising only a fraction of day care arrangements nationwide. Infant-toddler slots will take longer to get than slots for children over two years old.

The time to start looking for in-home care will depend upon whether the caregiver will be someone you already know, or someone you must find. If it's going to be a relative, for example, you may simply need to clear a start date with her. If you're planning to find a live-in housekeeper, start at least two months in advance; six months, if you expect to get someone from overseas. (You'll need at least that much time for overseas mailings of inquiries and reference checks, processing visas and working papers, et cetera). If you intend to have a "come-in" caregiver, one month in advance is probably enough time.

If you plan to use family day care, you should probably start looking about one month in advance (or more, to be on the safe side). You can adjust your timing based on information from friends on how long it took them, the amount of time you can spare for looking, or on the availability of family day care in your area. Family day care mothers tend to be concentrated in areas with lots of children, not too many very senior citizens, not too many very rich folk. If you have someone particular in mind, speak with her as early as you can and get her projections for how many kids she'll be caring for in the coming months. She will appreciate knowing, and may be able to hold a slot open for you.

Family day care networks sometimes have waiting lists. One common drawback to these waiting lists is that they are often for the network as a whole, not for individual day care mothers. You may have little control over who will have an opening when your number comes up. On the other hand, depending on other day care referral resources in your community, it's an alternative that may be well worth pursuing.

Make a tentative phone call or two (I'll tell you where in a minute) about eight months ahead of time to familiarize yourself with the child care situation in your locale. Based on the information you get, you can arrive at a ball-park figure for how far ahead of time you will need to plan for day care.

WHERE TO START LOOKING FOR DAY CARE

You're going to spend a lot of money on day care in the next few years. (You'll think the taxes that you pay for public education are a real deal by the time this is over!) What do you need to do? First, you need to become apprised of the various child care referral agencies that exist in your area.

State-Level Child Care Referral

All but two states (Florida and Mississippi) regulate some form of day care in some way. Therefore, you can almost always start with the state day care regulatory agency. They know at least where the day care they regulate is located. In addition, these agencies have often prepared consumer information pamphlets and/or lists of county child care referral services in that state. Usually it is possible to zero in on a more local day care referral service on the first pass, but the state agencies are good places to call or write if you know nothing about the child care resources in your community. There is a list of state day care licensing and referral agencies in Appendix A. Included are the agency's address, and phone number if available. This list of state day care agencies gives everyone somewhere to start. However, in most areas, there are ways of finding more local child care referral information.

The Yellow Pages

Many locales have child care information and referral agencies. These may be run by the city, town, or county, or may be private, nonprofit organizations. Look in your phone book for "Child-Care Referral," or under the name of your city, town, or county for "Child-Care Referral." Or call the city hall or county seat information number and ask about such an agency. In some areas, the public library serves as a clearinghouse for people wishing to list their availability as day care providers. Some communities have computerized systems that can be used to update such records continually. Private, nonprofit child care referral agencies may be listed in the Yellow Pages under "Child Care." These types of child care referral agencies often have names that include words such as *switchboard, hotline,* or *network* in the title.

Day care centers and day care home networks are also sometimes listed in the phone book under "Child Care." Do not take the list in the phone book to represent all the centers in your community. Frequently, centers run by school districts, or private or religious or other organizations do not have their own phone number, and so are not separately listed. Sometimes I think that private, run-for-profit day care centers get most of their inquiries simply because they are listed in the Yellow Pages, while the public and nonprofit centers are not.

Child Care Information and Referral Agencies

Child care information and referral agencies (I&Rs) usually serve two purposes. First, they keep lists of licensed child care in the area and try to match children to openings in these places. Second, they often administer subsidies for income-eligible families who may receive preferential placement in publicly funded day care slots. In locales with substantial lower-class populations, these agencies may be of limited usefulness to more middle-class families, since they are obligated by various regulations to try to spend their subsidy money on licensed day care slots for eligible families.

One drawback to many I&Rs is that since they receive public

money to disburse as child care subsidy, they must refer to only licensed or registered care. This is a real boondoggle, especially if you're looking for family day care, which much more often than not is unlicensed.

Sometimes these agencies do have lists of potential in-home caregivers. If your state doesn't regulate in-home care (and most do not) the agencies don't have to worry about referring nonlicensed caregivers for work in your home. More comprehensive I&Rs may have initially screened prospective in-home caregivers and checked out their references. Getting names of in-home caregivers from an I&R will be an efficient use of time, compared to advertising on your own. (Of course, initial screening by an I&R is no guarantee of anything!) However, most I&Rs have no listing of in-home providers.

Some I&Rs may help you arrange in-home "share care" (the type of arrangement where you and a few other families hire one caregiver for two to four babies, and the caregiver alternates among your homes). If you want to find a share-care arrangement, an I&R might be able to give you the names of other mothers as well as names of prospective caregivers.

I&Rs are always worth calling if they exist in your area, since the people there will have a good picture of day care resources in your area. In addition, I&Rs sometimes run services such as toy-loan libraries, working-parent colloquia, and caregiver training workshops.

Child care I&R agencies are the best source of specific, local information about available child care. But some communities have them and some don't. In addition, they have limitations, which I've already mentioned. Therefore, you should look beyond them, even if the one in your community seems to offer a large number of alternatives.

Child Care Referral through Community-Assistance Agencies

Some communities don't have referral agencies solely for child care. Child care referral services may be offered along with related family services by a social-service, community-development, child-development, or family-planning agency. If you check in your phone book under "Social Services," you'll find out exactly how these agencies in your community are listed. When you call, be sure to ask whether they know other agencies that make child care referrals, as well as asking whether they make child care referrals themselves.

In addition to public social-service agencies, there are private agencies that may be able to help you find day care. Examples of these are national family and youth organizations, such as the YMCA, the Red Cross, or Jewish Community Council. In some communities, these organizations may run their own day care programs or have programs they help support. If they don't, they may know other similar organizations that do.

Child Care Referral through Religious Organizations

Religious organizations may make child care referrals on a formal or informal basis. Checking with your local church or synagogue may be an especially good idea for you, if you're interested in a day care arrangement that teaches your child about aspects of your religion.

Often, private nonprofit (nonsectarian) and public day care centers happen to be housed in classroom wings of churches. Church classrooms make ideal day care centers because they are only used on Sundays. When you call a church, you may find that they know about a day care center because it is located on their premises, or at another church of their denomination.

Private Employment Agencies for Domestic Help

Some employment agencies specialize in the placement of child care workers and household domestics. These agencies are usually located in cities, although they may make placements for the surrounding suburbs as well. To find these agencies, you'll need to look in the phone book under "Employment Agencies" or "Domestic Help." Read the descriptions of services by each agency and call ones that look promising. You don't want a "temporary" as a caregiver, so don't call agencies that only do temporary placements.

These agencies are mostly useful to those of you looking for an in-home caregiver, especially one who would do both housework and child care. When you locate a potential caregiver through such an agency, be prepared to pay at least minimum wage. The employment counselor at the agency should be able to give you an idea of what salary you can expect to pay, before you begin talking with prospective caregivers.

Ask what the agency does in the way of screening before putting a prospective caregiver on its list. Ask whether the agency bonds its caregivers. Some agencies take a one-time fee from you and/or the employee for its services, and you become the employer. Other domestic-help employment agencies work on a commission basis and may handle paying the employee while you pay the agency. This latter procedure may be somewhat more costly, but will save you some hassling at tax time (see chapter two, the Child Care Tax Credit).

A small number of agencies, usually located in major cities, specialize in importing domestic and child care help from other countries for live-in arrangements. If you want such a live-in caregiver, using a private employment agency is probably the most efficient way to make these arrangements. They will manage the immigration paperwork and know the procedures.

Finding Child Care through Schools and Colleges

There is a growing movement in the United States for public day care facilities to be run by school districts or school systems on the premises of elementary schools. This is currently being done in areas where there are empty classrooms because of declining enrollment, and federal Title XX funds are being used to subsidize care through a state department of education. There is a rising proportion of preschoolers in need of day care, compared to children of school age. This means that classrooms once used for the elementary grades now stand empty. As school districts put one and one together, they begin to realize that it makes good fiscal sense to allocate empty classrooms for day care centers. School districts are especially inclined to run day care centers for three- to five-year-olds. Some of these programs may include a Head Start curriculum for at least half of the day.

Even if your local school system does not support any day care, chances are it will know which public agency does. Some school systems that do not play a part in public day care may still have day care on their premises. In some communities, it is permissible to rent unused classrooms (or whole schools) to private day care operators. Elementary school districts often use classroom space or other school facilities for after-school child care programs for school-age children.

Colleges and universities often maintain day care referral services. Sometimes these services are just for enrolled students, but sometimes colleges offer day care referral services to the general community. If you are a college student, graduate student, university affiliate, or faculty member, you may find that your college has special day care referral and day care facilities that you are eligible to use. College or university day care referral can usually be located by calling your campus information number, student union, or student-services center. Advantages of college-based day care include having your child nearby while you work or take classes, and possible subsidy if you are a student.

College child care referral is not the only child care resource that many campuses offer. If a campus includes student residences or a nearby "student ghetto" these are prime areas to find family day care mothers. These are areas with many young families in which the wife needs to earn some money while the husband goes to school. Often, these families have young children of their own. One way of finding family day care mothers in areas with heavy student populations is to place notices at the campus center or advertisements in nearby community centers, parks, or markets.

Advertising for Day Care

Locating child care information and referral agencies by making telephone calls is one approach to finding day care alternatives.

Another approach is to have the day care find you. You can do this by writing an ad, either for a newspaper or bulletin board.

Newspaper advertisements are excellent ways to find family day care mothers and in-home caregivers. The day care professionals whom I've surveyed universally agreed that the newspaper was the number-one means of finding day care for people in each of their states. You also can look for ads placed in a newspaper by people or centers offering day care services.

Before you write an ad, look at ads. Get your local paper. Locate the child care advertisements (probably somewhere in the classified section). Sometimes "Child Care" or "Day Care" has its own section; other times it's under "Domestic/Household Help" or under "Nursery or Preschools." In states where they are serious about family day care licensing, neither a mother looking for day care nor an unlicensed family day care mother can advertise in the "Child Care" section (as though that will change anything!). If your state prohibits family day care mothers to advertise as such (i.e., in a section titled "Child Care"), they may list themselves under "Domestic Help."

While you've got your local paper open to the classified section, and are checking to see what child care ads are like, look first under the appropriate headings for day care mothers, in-home caregivers, or day care centers offering their services. That may give you some leads right away.

Next, look for ads that other mothers have placed. If you've considered a share-care arrangement, in which you share one caregiver with other mothers in your home or theirs, it might be worthwhile to call other mothers who are advertising for family day care or in-home care in the same part of town as you. Together, you may be able to search for an in-home caregiver.

Notice the wording and size of the ads for caregivers. These may give you ideas about how you want your ad to look. Here's information that you'll want to include in your advertisement:

- Child's age and sex
- The kind of day care you want — for in-home care: "In my home"; for family day care: "In your home"

- Number of hours per week — for example: "full time," or "2 days per week," or "Tuesdays and Thursdays"
- Start date
- Location — for example "south of mid-town"
- When/where to call

In addition, you may want to add one or two other bits of information that will sort out caregivers that you absolutely do not want to interview: "Older women preferred," or "Woman with children preferred," "Must speak English well," "Must drive," and so on.

You may also want to add a little something extra that describes you, your child, or your concerns: "Loving care in your home," "Day care in your Christian home," "Energetic caregiver," "Care wanted for active twins," or even "Nonsmokers only."

Your newspaper advertisement should be brief. Call the paper before you start to work on an ad, and figure out the number of letters or lines you'll want to use for your message. Call back when you have it all together. Newspapers usually give you a choice of running an ad for one or more single days; or some sort of deal on one week or more. Two or three days is usually plenty of time. You can always opt for more days later. (You'll probably get some calls for a few days after the ad has been stopped anyway.) Ten or more responses per day is not unusual.

If you really don't want to have your phone ringing off the hook with responses to your newspaper ad, and you have some lead time, you can arrange to have inquiries sent to a newspaper box number. (This will discourage some prospects, but hopefully not the best ones.) Then you can pick up your responses and answer them when you are ready.

If you plan to put ads on bulletin boards as well, you'll probably want to prepare a more expanded version of the information that went into your newspaper ad. Although bulletin boards are usually free, and newspaper advertising is not, you can expect the newspaper ad to give you quicker, more frequent responses. You'll want to put a "date posted" line on a bulletin board ad so potential callers will know if you're still likely to be looking.

You may also want to add a little eye-catching cartoon of a baby, toddler, or stroller to your bulletin board ad so the right people will pick it out from other ads for different things. Try a format that has your phone number on fringed strips hanging from the bottom. Or you may want your ad to have a pocket attached to it; then put cards with your number in that.

One nice thing about bulletin board ads is that you can narrow your audience a bit. Depending on your own lifestyle, you might want to put ads up at the local "alternative lifestyles" bookstore, the natural-foods cooperative grocery store, or the natural childbirth resource and referral center.

Word-of-Mouth Child Care Referral

Undoubtedly the easiest possible way to find day care is to ask your best friend what she does and then do the same thing. Assuming that two friends understand each other's values and each other's children, this might seem to be an ideal way to find day care. However, this is frequently not the case. Asking about day care arrangements among your friends and co-workers (and among your spouse's friends and co-workers) is one of the good, initial ways to get a handle on day care in your community. Multiple independent recommendations can be good pointers toward a fine day care arrangement.

When people recommend a day care arrangement to you, be sure to differentiate between day care that they've heard about and day care that they've actually seen. Often people name day care centers they have never been to. A day care center located at the intersection of two busy streets that you and ten people you know pass on the way to work each day is an unknown quantity, except for its convenient location.

If someone tells you that she has a great day care arrangement, ask her to tell you about it, and why she likes it. Try to have your friend describe the arrangement in objective terms.

The biggest problem with word-of-mouth referral is that everyone wants to tell you what is right about the way they are raising their child. Someone with a mediocre-to-poor day care arrangement might even recommend it to you in order consciously or unconsciously to allay her own apprehensions about its inadequacies. Caveat emptor.

Word-of-mouth referral certainly is the best way to end up sharing a day care arrangement with someone you know. In family day care, or in-home share-care, problems can arise over conflicting needs of different parents. This may be especially difficult to handle if you find yourself compromising your needs for the sake of your friendship; for example, taking day care on for Monday, Wednesday, and Thursday mornings, because that's what your friend wants, when you'd rather have Monday, Wednesday, and Friday mornings. On the other hand, it may be easier for you to communicate about problems with a day care arrangement with someone you know, rather than with someone that you don't know.

There may also be problems arising from feelings of possessiveness on the part of the first family using a care arrangement when you (the second family) start your child later. Otherwise sensible people can get quite strange when it comes to their children.

If you already use day care and need to change arrangements (if, for example, the day care mother is "going out of business"), you may want to ask other families with whom you share the arrangement what they plan to do. Since these are people who seem to value the same choices in day care as you, they may have good ideas of where to look next.

Chapter 5

Assessing Day Care:
How to Interview and Observe

YOU HAVE FOUND THE NAMES of prospective caregivers or day care centers. You are ready to begin evaluating these potential arrangements. What will you need to do?

No matter which type of day care you select, a phone interview should be your first step. Next, schedule a personal interview with candidates that pass the phone screening at the place of care — whether in your home, their home, or the day care center. Third, you'll need to decide on an arrangement, and call back to let each candidate know your decision. Those are the bare bones of the process.

This chapter will focus on issues to discuss with prospective caregivers, how to discuss them, and when to discuss them. The steps for interviewing and observing in either type of home-based care are similar because in both cases you will be concerned with the one caregiver: what she will do, and how she will run things. When evaluating day care centers, on the other hand, you're likely to have an initial contact with the director. Then, when you go for a visit, you will want to observe; you won't be as interested in the director herself, as in what she can show you about her staff, the program, curriculum, philosophy, or routine.

For in-home care, you should plan to hold, at the very least, three interviews in your home. You should speak with at least five candidates on the phone so you know what's out there. More than three home interviews would be especially appropriate if you never before have had help in your home. The more people you interview, the better the idea you will have of what you can expect and what it will cost.

If your problem is too many possibilities, limit the number you see by more careful phone screening, and visits that can be scheduled at your convenience. It is helpful to make all phone calls and, later, all interviews, on the same day or in the same week. That way, all your impressions will be fresh, and your decisions will be based on clear recollections.

For family day care, you should plan to visit *at least* three day care homes, probably five at the most. Some parents visit ten or more. Keep making visits until you find one that feels right. If you have never been to a family day care home before, I suggest that you visit at least three homes just to formulate a basis for comparison. It might even be worth your while to visit a home that sounds unsuitable over the phone. Then you can compare that home to ones that sound better. It really is essential that you visit more than one day care home. If you don't, you will have no way of knowing what you might be missing.

THE TELEPHONE INTERVIEW

A phone interview is a good opportunity to gather information and form a first impression while not having to commit yourself to any further interchanges with that caregiver. This will be your best opportunity to be an impartial judge of a caregiver's qualifications. Here are a few things to keep in mind when you first speak with a caregiver:

- Your initial phone screening will go most smoothly if you adopt an agenda and stick to it.
- You have the right to any information that might affect your child's well-being.
- Remember that you are in charge of the conversation.
- Make sure that you get complete, satisfactory answers to all your questions.

- If the conversation strays too far afield, don't hesitate to reinitiate your topic.
- If it is clear that you are speaking with a caregiver whom you'll not be able to use, feel free to end the conversation politely. There is no reason to waste either your time or hers.

It might help to role-play, or rehearse, the questions with your spouse or a friend. (They might even have suggestions for additional questions to include, based on their knowledge of your child.) Once you become comfortable with an interview format, you should find that even awkward issues such as salary can be discussed with a minimum of discomfort.

Here is a sample phone interview. If you use this interview or devise one like it, you'll be assured of getting your basic questions answered. Using a written-down interview format will help you remember who said what. You can make copies of this phone interview and keep them handy.

Telephone Screening for In-Home Caregivers

Introduce yourself. State your child's name, age, and sex. Make it clear when you'll need day care. If you are calling her, tell her how you got her name.

- Caregiver's name _____
- Telephone number _____
  Best time to call _____
- Address _____
- How much previous experience have you had taking care of children? *Much* ☐ *Some* ☐ *None* ☐
  Has lived in? *Yes* ☐ *No* ☐
- How long have you been taking care of children?
  _____months *or* _____years
- How many families have you worked for? _____
- How long do you plan to continue doing child care for a living? _____
- Do you do housework? *Yes* ☐ *No* ☐ (*If yes, check those that apply.*)

—Light housework: *Kitchen cleanup* □ *Making beds* □
  Laundry □ *Vacuuming* □
—Heavier chores: *Washing floors* □ *Windows* □ *Shopping* □
  Gardening □
• Can you arrange your own transportation? *Yes* □ *No* □
  Do you have your own car? *Yes* □ *No* □
• What hours of the day are you available? _____
  How do you charge? *Hourly* □ *Daily* □ *Weekly* □
  How much do you charge? (*Be prepared to state the approximate
  salary you would offer.*) _____
• Could you please provide me with two references?
  Name and number _____
  Name and number _____
• Appointment for interview:
  Day of the week _____
  Date _____ Time _____

Telephone Screening of Family Day Care Mothers

*Introduce yourself. State your child's name, age, and sex. Make it clear
when you'll need day care.*

• Family day care mother's name _____
• Telephone number _____
  Best time to call _____
• Address _____
• Do you care for any children at the present time?
    Yes □ *No* □ (*If yes:*)
    Your own children? *Yes* □ *No* □
      Ages and sexes _____
    Day care children? *Yes* □ *No* □
      Ages and sexes _____
    How many children full time? _____
    How many children part time? _____
• How long have you had a day care home? _____
• How long do you plan to continue this work? _____
• How do the children spend their time at your home?
  (*Remember to probe for complete answers.*)
    Indoor play? (*Hours per day*) _____

Outdoor play? (*Hours per day*) ————————
TV? (*Hours per day*) ————————————
Meals/Snacks? ————— Included in fee? *Yes* □ *No* □
Napping arrangements? ——————————————
Where do the children play? ——————————
What kinds of toys do you have? ——————————
- (*Ask about any special needs for your child, such as transportation to nursery school or administering medications.*)
- How do you charge? *Hourly* □ *Daily* □ *Weekly* □
  How much do you charge? ————————————
- Could you please provide me with two references?
  Name and number ——————————————
  Name and number ——————————————
- Appointment for interview:
  Day of the week ——————————————
  Date ——— Time ———

Screening Techniques

The first thing to do when a prospective caregiver calls, or when you call her, is to introduce yourself, describe your child, and briefly state your day care needs. If you are calling her, you should state how you got her name. Make sure that it is a convenient time for both of you to talk.

The central purpose of the initial phone contact is to judge whether it is even logistically possible to discuss a day care arrangement. Don't get excited about a possible day care arrangement until you know whether this caregiver will be available. Most of the items on the initial phone interview address those practical issues.

If it might be possible to have a day care arrangement with this caregiver (she's ready to start, she's willing to take care of a child the age of your child), it's time to get a feeling for this woman's personality. However, it's not necessary to focus on much more than the practical issues during your first contact. Some topics are best discussed during a face-to-face interview.

I don't like to make judgments about people over the phone because some people sound much more competent than they really are, while other people are unduly nervous.

Some of the questions that need to be asked initially will require probing. Being a good, objective prober is the key to being a successful interviewer. For example, you will probably have to probe a bit to find out what the daily schedule of the children in the day care home is, or will be. You will have to probe an in-home caregiver to determine how close her previous work experience has been to the job you have in mind for her. When interviewing a day care center director on the phone, you may have to probe to find out what the program is.

Questions that you devise to elicit information should always be phrased in a nondirective, value-free way. Don't provide leading statements; that is, try not to phrase questions in a way that implies the answer. Don't let on what you believe to be the "right" or "wrong" way of child-rearing. Of course, you need to find a caregiver who shares your ideas about children, but stating your ideas and then asking if she agrees is not the way to get an accurate answer. Do allow enough pauses in the conversation to get the caregiver's point of view. Caregivers will have different philosophies. But they may tell you what you want to hear in their eagerness to please or in order to create business for themselves. Either way, a suggestive question may preclude your receiving an honest answer.

Try not to dwell on your view of any child-rearing issues during this initial screening. Instead, try to draw out the caregiver's points of view. Phrase questions so that a variety of responses will seem acceptable. By giving a caregiver the latitude to express her views, you will learn about her values. You may even hear some very sound reasoning you hadn't considered!

Here are some examples and counterexamples demonstrating what I mean by nondirective, value-free phrasing:

DO ASK: How do you get children down for a nap?
DON'T ASK: Do all the children take their naps at the same time each day?
WORSE YET: You keep naps on a schedule, don't you?

DO ASK: What did you do when you potty-trained your
               four-year-old?
DON'T ASK: I've been giving my daughter candies when she
               goes to the potty. Do you do it that way too?

It may seem obvious that you don't want to provide prompts for the answers that you would like to hear. However, if you are anxious about settling on a day care arrangement, and that is often the case, you may unconsciously be trying to hurry the difficult process of selecting a caregiver by cueing her to say what you want to hear. (Please don't confuse avoiding "leading questions" with your right to specify how you want the caregiver you *do* choose to do things. Right now, you just want to locate someone who is in the same ball park as you are, in terms of child-rearing philosophy.)

During the initial phone interview, you should focus not so much on *what* is said, but on *how* it is said. Does this person sound intelligent? (You don't have to be well educated to be intelligent.) Do you feel awkward because of the way this person responds? Does she seem to listen to your questions or only speak her own agenda? Does she seem to be someone you would like to meet?

THE PERSONAL INTERVIEW

Once you've completed several phone interviews, or run out of time to do more initial screening, you'll be ready to move on to the next stage of the selection process: deciding whom to see in person and in which order. The most efficient way of doing this is to sort your prospective care arrangements into three categories, based on your talks with them on the phone.

The first category would consist of the most likely candidates — caregivers or centers with whom you made appointments at the end of your phone interview.

The second category would be your "wait-and-sees." Sometimes it's not easy to tell what someone's like on the phone. Nervousness or an inconvenient moment for a phone call can cause the caregiver to give you an inaccurate first impression. There may have been some logistical inconvenience (for example, not having her own car to do after-school runs) that made you want to wait and see if a more practical arrangement would turn up.

Early on, it will be hard to get a feel for arrangements you'll eventually want to consider seriously, since you will have had a small basis for comparison so far. Your second category of caregivers, then, will also include those whom you told you would call back as soon as you started making decisions about personal interviews.

In the third category are those who will definitely not work out. Included in this category is the one who simply lived too far away and the one who couldn't accommodate your working hours. This category also includes the woman who screamed at her kids and didn't even put her hand over the phone, and the pregnant sixteen-year-old who had done a lot of babysitting. In the third category are those who should have been thanked for their interest and told "No, thank you" during your initial screening.

You will be surprised at how easy it is to give a polite "no, thank you." Here are some easy-to-follow scripts for saying it: "Thank you for calling, but I really need to find someone closer to where I live (work)"; or "Thank you, I really am glad you followed up on my ad, but I'm fairly certain I'll be taking my daughter to another woman I spoke with yesterday"; or, to the persistent caller who won't let you off the phone, "I'm glad we've talked, but my baby's beginning to fuss. Thank you. Good-bye."

Once you've finished categorizing your possibilities, you can call back those in the second category and either make an appointment to visit their homes or have them visit you, or let them know that you are no longer interested.

When you make appointments for visits, there are a few things to keep in mind:

- You should allow at least one hour for each visit.
- Always bring your own child no matter how young she is. (If you are pregnant, this will be no extra effort.)
- Plan to go at a time when your child is not sleepy or hungry (if possible!).

- For family day care or center day care, if the caregiver or director stalls on arranging a visit, or having you come when the children are around, or awake, be cautious.
- For in-home care, if the caregiver hesitates to make an appointment with you, or to muster the resources to try and figure out how she'll get to your house, be cautious. This may not be the job she really wants.

It's ideal for both mothers and fathers to participate in interviewing caregivers or visiting day care centers. Day care is family business. Often, parents alternate in dropping off the child in the mornings and picking her up at the end of the day. It should be an arrangement that will work for both of you, as well as for your child. Realistically, fathers are often working when these interviews take place. If the father can't be there, he should be kept abreast of all that's happening and be given an opportunity to help decide, albeit based on the mother's reports. (If, as a father, your time is limited, you might want to hold back on visiting until it seems like the time for a final decision.)

The purpose of interviewing in person is to see what the prospective caregiver is really like. You want to see whether you will be able to get along with her. Remember that you are not looking simply for someone who agrees with everything you say. You will want someone who will be able to acknowledge your right to decide how your children should be raised, but still be able to make most decisions on her own.

For most people, an interview with a prospective caregiver or a visit to a day care center can be an exhausting experience. You have to be friendly, and simultaneously show that you know what you want, and that you have questions that you intend to have answered. There are two techniques you can use to help you juggle the various goals of your interview. The first technique is the open-ended interview. Open-ended interviewing is the best way to get the facts that you'll need to decide about the caregiver's capabilities. The second technique is unobtrusive observation. This form of observation is a way of keeping track of the underlying message, the hidden agenda, that is being communicated.

Open-ended Interviewing: How to Get at Child-rearing Values and Attitudes

The purpose of open-ended interviewing is to pose questions that do not necessarily have right or wrong answers, but that provide information about a person's values. You need to know what the caregiver is like as a caregiver, as well as what she is like as a person. The same goes for day care centers. You should have an opportunity to chat with the staff as individuals, not just watch them from a distance. You will be relating to your child's caregiver(s) every day that she is in day care, so your personal feelings count too.

When you arrive at a day care home or center, introduce yourself and your child. If you are interviewing an in-home caregiver in your home, have your child with you, and let him be in the room while you talk. Start off by offering some coffee or tea.

If a day care mother or center director offers you coffee, accept it. Starting out informally should put you both at ease. The purpose of your visit is to see if you can establish a work relationship; the type of distancing you may be accustomed to in employer/employee relations just isn't appropriate with someone who will take care of your child.

If you are a professional woman, try not to dress the part for these interviews. Your silk suit from Saks may impress your clients, but will probably make someone who is dressed to work with little children feel uncomfortable and unnecessarily inferior.

If your child is old enough to crawl or walk, put her down. See where she goes, and how she reacts to the caregiver and any other children. If your child clings to your leg during the whole interview, please realize that this is quite a normal expression of wariness of unfamiliar adults. Children vary a great deal in their tendency to explore a strange situation.

Once you and your child are comfortably situated, you can go ahead with the interview. Be conversational. You'll want to flesh out several of the questions you asked on the phone. For example: "You mentioned that you only take care of one- and two-year-olds. What is it that you like about that age group?" Or, "On the phone you asked me whether Timmy has been with other children before.

Do you think that's important? Why?" Ask as many questions as you can that require more than a simple yes or no.

Tell a prospective day care mother or housekeeper that you'd like to begin by getting a picture of how she feels about her own children and the children she has had in her care. Ask a center director how long it has been since she started working with children. If you begin by showing an interest in her (while still getting information *you* need), you'll break the ice, and things will go smoothly. Here are some good starters, topics you'll probably want to cover:

- What kinds of personalities do the children here have? Or, What kinds of kids have you cared for?
- How did you get into taking care of kids?
- What do you find most difficult in raising children?

Take the time necessary to establish good rapport. Add your own opinions to hers and see how she reacts. Does she change her mind about her point of view if she sees that it doesn't agree with yours? (It shouldn't if it is well thought out.) Notice the emotional tone of the words she uses in referring to her children.

Remember that your interview is taking place while the day care mother or center director is "at work." It is a positive sign if your conversation is occasionally interrupted so she can pay necessary attention to children.

Phrase questions generally, and in a way that allows for extended comment. Let the person you are interviewing offer complete answers. Avoid interrupting or interjecting, so that the interviewee can continue talking until she has said all she feels there is to say (in contrast to stopping when she thinks you've heard enough). The more people talk about one issue, the less constrained and superficial the response becomes. One long answer may reveal more about the way a person reasons and feels than many short answers.

This is the time to ask questions about substantive issues. Here are some questions you may want to ask:

- What kinds of things do you do to help a new child adjust to his mother's leaving him for the first time? What do you do when children cry because they miss their parents? (*Probe for her strategies for dealing with a child's separation anxiety, intermittent crying during the day. What does she say to the child, what does she do for him?*)

- What do you do about discipline? What kinds of rewards and punishments do you use? (*Avoid those who spank or isolate severely.*)
- What are your policies about bottle-weaning? Toilet-training? Pacifiers? Demand feedings? (*Avoid those who are much more restrictive or much more permissive about these things than you are.*)

Additional questions for home-based caregivers (all of these may not apply to your situation):

- How does your husband feel about your working? About your doing child care? Is your husband or other adults home during the day? Does he do things with children? (*Does he view day care as a transitional job he'll soon encourage her to quit? Will he expect her to take days off whenever he has days off?*)
- What is your plan for when you are sick or on vacation? (*Will this meet your needs?*)
- Why have you decided to start taking care of children? *Or,* Why did you stop your last job? How did you feel about the people you used to work for? What did you like and dislike about working for them?
- Why have you decided to take on another child at this point? How many children would you ideally like to be taking care of?

Additional questions for group care — family day care and center day care (again, all of these may not apply to your situation):

- Where are the children allowed to play? What do you do about play space in the winter? (*For family day care, the run of the house is nicest, one room off-limits is OK, restriction to one or two rooms is not as good. Centers should have extra room for wintertime play if it's too cold to go out.*)
- Which are the children's favorite toys? (*Are there enough of the favorites or do they have to be rationed?*)

- What are your arrangements about meals? Snacks? (*Are they provided? Is there a convenient place to feed children?*)
- What's the procedure for naptime? (*Separate rooms are great, one room for all is OK, sleeping where and while others play is no good.*)
- What is your sick-child policy? (*Will it meet your needs?*)

Develop a picture of how your child will spend his time. Ask questions to complete your picture. Does the person you are interviewing seem to really love children? Or, is this just a job? Avoid the latter! Another task during the open-ended interviewing is to determine the child-rearing values of the caregiver or the center: where would you place her (it) on the continuum from laissez-faire to authoritarian, which we discussed in the first chapter? Remember that the research shows that the more nearly the caregiver's views correspond to your own, the better the arrangement is likely to work out.

After you finish with these questions, you may want to try another interviewing technique: getting reactions to hypothetical situations by describing a possible event and asking the caregiver how she would react if that event really happened. For example, ask, "How would you react if you saw Jason pulling the baby's hair?" Or ask, "What could you do if you saw that Jennifer developed a bad habit, say, putting things in her ears, and the other children began to copy her?" How does she deal with parents: "What would you say to Beth's mother if she kept bringing her when she had a fever, even though her mother knew your policy is for parents to keep sick children at home?"

Caregivers may feel more comfortable with questions phrased as hypothetical situations. Presenting a hypothetical situation may remind some caregivers of things that really happened, and how they handled them.

You will also need to clarify nitty-gritty issues that may influence whether all aspects of the day care arrangement will be functional. You'll need to negotiate hours, meals, transportation, et cetera. Discussion of these practical concerns should be reserved for the latter part of the visit. (You will have clarified major logistical issues over the telephone.) When you begin to make arrangements, it's best to just state what you ideally want and take it from there. Try some give and take. If the caregiver or center really can't take your child earlier than 9:00, and you need day care from 8:30 on, maybe you can pick him up a half hour later and move your work day up by half an hour.

When you begin to ask such practical questions at the end of the visit, you are, in effect, signaling the caregiver or director that you think you will be able to work out an arrangement. If you are sure the caregiver or center you are considering isn't going to work out, don't even bother to bring up these topics.

Unobtrusive Observation

While the two of you talk, you will have a chance to see the caregiver in action. If you are at her home, you will get to see how well she deals with any children of her own, and the children she already cares for, plus your own child. If she's at your house, you can see how comfortable she seems in your surroundings and how well she "takes" to your child. If you are at a center, try to arrange to do your talking in a room full of kids, rather than in the director's office. The more you can compare what they say to what you see, the better able you will be to make a judgment about that potential arrangement.

The idea behind this kind of observation, called unobtrusive observation, is to interpret what you see happening around you while you are talking about other things. You will learn different things about a way a person does things if they don't think they are being directly observed. Pay particular attention to whether a caregiver's actions agree with what she has been saying. Does the way she *treats* children seem in line with the way she *talks* about them? What do her actions tell you about her satisfaction with her work? For example, when a caregiver takes a child from place to place, does she just hold him in a routine manner, or does she look at and talk to the child all the while? Are older children led by the wrist, or does the caregiver really hold hands?

The children in the day care setting also provide clues about what goes on there. Listen to what they say. Watch how they act with one another. How well do they relate to the caregiver? Do they see her as a friend? If an in-home caregiver brings her own children along, or a family day care mother has her own kids at home, watch these children in particular. Check out how loving or fearful, how intimate or distant, how dependent or independent they seem to be.

Asking a family day care mother about her children is equivalent to asking an applicant for some other type of job about her work experiences. You may want to ask the caregiver whether she has had any out-of-home work experience with children.

Does the caregiver seem energetic or tired when attending to a child? Do her actions seem tailored to exactly what the child is communicating, or do they seem routine? Does she seem to be particularly enthusiastic about your child, or does she convey the attitude that all children are the same? Does she speak fondly of other children she's cared for, and tell you little anecdotes about them? You may find this boring, but it shows that she has felt an attachment to each of these children. You would want her to talk about your child that way if she took care of him.

Here's a list of the most important questions to ask yourself while conducting a personal interview with a prospective caregiver or center director:

- Does the caregiver/head teacher ask to hold your child or try to talk to or play with him? (A good sign.)
- Does your child seem to like the caregiver(s)? What exactly does he do or not do to give you that impression? (Remember to take into account how your child usually reacts to strangers.)
- Do you feel comfortable in the caregiver's/teacher's company? (Don't minimize the importance of this.)
- Is the home or center well-kept? (Compulsive neatness may mean not enough time spent with the children; but the place should be presentable.)
- Does the caregiver stop attending to the children because you (an adult) are there? (Ideally not.)
- Does the caregiver/teacher try to involve your child with the other children? (Rate this highly.)
- Do the children there seem happy and at ease? (Not made uncomfortable by your presence?)
- Do the children seem to mix well together? (Remember

that children under two years old do not typically play together.)
- Is television being used as a babysitter? (Some TV, for example, educational, age-appropriate programs, is OK.)
- Does the family day care mother show preferential treatment for her children over the day care children? (Ideally
not.)
- Is the day care home child-proof? (Check the cabinets for
child-proof latches, electrical outlets for plugs, etc. There
shouldn't be too many breakable items within reach.)

The best way to pace your visit is to conclude your interview and
observation simultaneously. You may, however, run out of questions before you feel you've seen enough. In that case, don't hesitate to ask if it's all right to just sit and watch how your child be-
haves in this setting for a little while longer.

Toward the end of the visit, you may want to ask the caregiver
or head teacher how she feels your child would fit into her group or
what she thinks it would be like to take care of your child. By this
time, she will have had an opportunity to observe your child. Does
what she say match what you would expect?

One nice way of ending a visit is to tour any parts of the home or
outdoor play area that you have not already seen together. In family day care, a tour is especially important, so that you can see just
how much space there is for the children. State laws regulate play
space in day care centers.

An in-home caregiver will want to see all of *your* house, especially
if she is going to live in. If she will do housework, assessing the size
of your home will be part of what she needs to do in order to decide
whether she wants your job.

Make sure you have all the information you wanted before ending the visit. If you have a written checklist of questions and things
to observe during the interview, and I suggest you do, this is the
time to go back over it. If you find that you have forgotten to ask
something, ask now.

At the end of each interview, you'll have many details swimming around in your head. It's admittedly quite difficult to assign
a value to everything you've heard and observed, and come up
with an overall evaluation of the care arrangement. After each in-

terview is over there are the three major questions you should ask yourself. A yes answer to all three should be mandatory for any further consideration of the care arrangement:

- Does this person have the necessary intelligence and skills to take care of a child properly? For a center, does the total staff provide responsive care?
- Do you find the caregiver or center staff members you would deal with to be personable?
- Do the caregiver(s) and your child hit it off?

As you conclude the interview, you will have to say something about your decision-making process. Do not allow yourself to be pressured by the caregiver or by the center director. Centers and family day care homes sometimes try to demonstrate their value as a precious commodity by telling you about their waiting lists, or how much parents are willing to pay for their service. The ultimate day care "con" line is: "I really didn't plan to take any more children, but Johnny is so cute that I'll make an exception if you want to start him right now." A good caregiver or center will give you at least twenty-four hours to make your decision.

One family who chose the first family day care home they saw, were convinced of its merits after being told of its waiting list, and that they would have to pay full fees for two weeks before they needed care, just to reserve a place. My question was, if there was a waiting list, what was this day care mother doing by interviewing and giving a place to a family not even on her list?

The point is that the caregiver or center may be just as eager as you are to resolve your child care dilemma. But it should be you, and not them, making the decision about your child.

What should you say as you conclude the interview? Be as truthful as possible, express any uncertainties that you have. Your comments should fit into one of these three categories: 1) You'd like to finalize arrangements. 2) You'll call her back. 3) It won't work out.

Here are some ways to give a fair appraisal of your impressions. For example: "I really like what you do with the children here. My husband and I are going to make a final decision tonight and I will call you in the morning." Another scenario: "I have appointments to visit three more homes. I'll call you Tuesday afternoon after I've finished those visits." For many people, it is easier to give bad news over the phone: "Thank you for coming to see me the other day, but I've found a woman who can work Saturday mornings, too."

By the time you have been through the steps of interviewing a number of caregivers or teachers by phone and in person, you'll have sufficient information to make your choice. If you have never used day care before, I can assure you that you will feel as though you have learned a great deal.

The information gathered during your visits provides you with a means of deciding what you want and what you can actually have. Some families tend to be overly flexible and choose the first thing that seems to fit the bill. They generate all sorts of obtuse reasons why a particular arrangement is desirable. "She has a lot of animals and we don't want him to grow up afraid of animals. Besides, she has a nursery school down the street and in another three years we could send him there." Other families may be overly sensitive to innuendo and small observations, and not be able to see the relative merits among the choices they have. The best advice at this point is to go with your feelings, more than with your rationalizations.

Please try not to make a final decision until you've made comparisons. Approach each potential care arrangement with an open mind. Discuss your feelings about each prospect with your spouse.

*Extra Steps in the Selection of a Day Care Center*___

In the preceding sections we have talked about selecting child care in general, and interviewing and observing caregivers in particular. Much of what was said in those sections applies no matter which type of child care you select. Day care centers are much more difficult to select than home-based caregivers. First of all, the "average" day care center often provides less than what I believe to be the minimum quality of care parents should be satisfied with. Second, a center has many different caregivers, each of whom must be evaluated separately. Third, day care centers are the least prevalent type of child care, and usually have the fewest openings. Their scarcity seems to make them more desirable to some parents. Here are some additional guidelines for gathering information about day care centers.

A good time of day to screen day care centers by telephone is about 12:30 to 1:00. Lunch is usually over and many children will be resting or napping. (Amazingly, day care centers can get twenty one- and two-year-olds all to go down for naps within fifteen minutes.) It's a time of day when the director or head teacher is least likely to have other unavoidable tasks. Large centers usually have full-time receptionists that can answer initial questions at any time of the day.

First, you will need to determine whether a given center is likely to have an opening when you will need it. If it doesn't, you'll need to find out about its waiting-list policy. You may want to arrange a visit to a center well before you need day care, so that you can decide whether you seriously would consider using that center, and whether you want to be on their waiting list.

If you're thinking, "What's the harm in being on as many waiting lists as I can," keep in mind that waiting lists provide you with an illusion of security that you are waiting for something you want. However, many good centers won't even put you on their list until you come for a visit. They don't want a waiting list that is falsely inflated with names of kids who are on ten other lists. Some centers require you to submit a nonrefundable deposit (which can later be applied to tuition, if you use the center).

Here's a common scenario having to do with day care waiting lists that you should try to avoid: Allison is one and a half and attends a center where she *could* stay until she is three years old. Knowing that it's difficult to find day care, Allison's mother, Janet, puts her on the waiting list for a preschool-age center. She's told the waiting list is one year long (not uncommon). Shortly after Allison turns two, Janet gets a call from the preschool-age center, telling her that after seven months on the waiting list, there is an opening for Allison. If she doesn't take it, she'll go to the bottom of the list, and wait up to a year all over again. Janet jumps at the chance, takes Allison from a center where she's perfectly happy, and puts her into an environment where she's about a year younger than almost all the other children.

Unfortunately, it's hard to help feeling that you've won something when you've waited a long time for it. It's also hard to take the chance of starting to wait again, when you don't have to wait anymore. Most people have an understandable tendency to take a sure thing instead of holding out for some uncertain thing in the future. Probably the single most common reason that parents choose a particular day care center *without* having seen any others is that it was the first one to have an opening.

That brings us to the good side of waiting lists. With good advance planning, playing the waiting-list game is the only way to get your child into a really excellent day care center.

Let's get back to Janet and her daughter Allison. I would like to have seen them visit several preschool centers before putting Allison's name on any waiting list. That way, when her name came up, Janet and her husband could have better weighed the merits of that center against others and against the chance of waiting for a slot at another center. She could have called the other centers and determined what position she was in with them.

A final word about waiting lists. If you consider publicly sponsored centers, you may find that your local referral agency or child care coordinating council maintains one waiting list for all the centers collectively. Mostly such systems are constructed by those who assume that only subsidized families will want public care and that "beggars can't be choosers." That attitude underrates the fine quality of many public centers, and the parents' ability to decide what is best for their own children.

When you first call a day care center, you may not be able to decide whether or not you want to visit. Wait until you've called several. Then call back the most appealing ones and make appointments to visit. One thing you should realize is that some centers that serve children three and over, and that run a preschool program along with extended day care, are closed during the summer. If you are a schoolteacher or a student, this may be OK with you. You may encounter problems when you want to visit such a nine-month center. Since they are closed in the summer, you'll need to make visits during the previous spring, if you want care the following fall or winter. It's difficult to get a true picture of what such a center is like by visiting in early fall, because the pace of things takes a while to establish itself for both staff and children. In addition, if you visit too far in advance, there may be so much staff and child turnover that things are qualitatively quite different by the time you actually need care.

There may be a center in your community that you have heard is *the* best. Even if it has an impossible waiting list, or costs far more than you can afford, it may be educational for you to visit it. You'll be able to see how good it is, and how other, perhaps less well-known, centers compare to it. If you really dislike the "good" center, it may be that center day care is not the right choice for you and your child.

If you live in a community with a university or college, it may run a lab day care center or preschool program. Remember that having someone use your child in a research study doesn't mean he's getting better-quality care. In fact, lab schools often employ trainee caregivers who may have less expertise than can be found elsewhere in your community.

Now that you know a few extra things about looking for center day care, you're ready to begin making calls to see what's available. Here's the initial information you should get from each center that you phone:

Telephone Screening of Day-Care Centers

Introduce yourself. State your child's name, age, and sex. Make it clear when you'll need day care.

- Name of the day care center _____
- Telephone number _____
  Best time to call _____
- Address _____
- Open year-round? *Yes* ☐ *No* ☐
- Closed on public-school holidays? *Yes* ☐ *No* ☐

lat is your sponsorship? *Public* ☐ *Private, Nonprofit* ☐ *Pri-
t, profit* ☐

- How many children are at your center? _____
- What is the age range of children at your center?

_____

- How many classrooms of children do you have? _____
- How many children full time? _____
- How many children part time? _____
- How many teachers are there? _____
  How many per class? _____
  How many teachers versus how many aides? _____
  What is your teacher-to-child ratio? _____
  (*It should be about 1:4 for under one year; 1:6 for 1–2 years;
  1:8–10 for 2–3 years; 1:12–14 over three years.*)
- Could you briefly describe your program? (*Remember to probe
  for complete answers.*)
  Indoor play? (*Hours per day*) _____
  Outdoor play? (*Hours per day*) _____
  Meals/Snacks? _____ Included in fee? *Yes* ☐ *No* ☐
  Napping arrangements? _____
- (*Ask about any special needs for your child, such as transportation to
  nursery school or administering medication.*)
- How do you charge? *Hourly* ☐ *Daily* ☐ *Weekly* ☐
  How much do you charge? _____
- Do you have any openings? *Yes* ☐ *No* ☐
  If no openings, do you have a waiting list? *Yes* ☐ *No* ☐
  How long is the waiting list? _____
  How long have the most recent families had to wait?

_____

- Appointment for interview:
  Day of the week _____
  Date _____ Time _____
  Whom to see _____ Title _____

You will call some centers where the phone rings eleven times
before the harried teacher picks up. Just because she doesn't have
time for a prolonged chat doesn't mean that the center is not a
good one. Staff in a small center that lacks a full-time administrator should pay more attention to children than to phone calls.

At other centers you may find that your inquiry produces a standardized stream of statements concerning the center's program, costs, and openings. While it is nicer for you to talk with a more conversational informant, it *is* difficult for them not to sound monotonous if they repeat the same message fifty times each week. Many centers receive literally hundreds of calls each month. A canned message from a receptionist doesn't necessarily mean that the individual classrooms won't be nice.

Some centers may have brochures describing their program and facilities. Ask them to mail you one. A little bit of advertising is a good way to summarize a program. I am apprehensive, however, about day care centers that will give you slick reams of many-colored sheets that detail the sundry aspects of the "Little Red School House" way to grow up. Of course, at most centers, you'll reach a real human being who will be eager to provide you with whatever information you want. I rate highly centers that respond that way.

If you reach the director or head teacher, you may find that she has a certain curiosity about you as well. She may try to place you as either a permissive or authoritarian parent, and then cast her center in those terms. For the permissive parent: "Yes, we encourage children to realize that they need their naps so they can get the most out of their afternoon experiences." For the authoritarian parent: "Yes, we believe that children need to learn that there is a time and a place for everything. That's why nap time is always at twelve-thirty, every day." A director may try to find out who you are: that is, where you and your spouse work, where any other kids of yours go to school, in which neighborhood you live, and to which community or religious organizations you belong. Don't be taken aback by these questions. If you use the center, they will find out all these things about you anyway. Consciously or unconsciously, the director or head teacher is trying to clarify for herself and for you how well you will fit into the group of families that uses that center. She knows that this fit can be important to how she'll get along with you, how the teachers will react to your child, and how happy you will be in choosing that center.

Some center directors may ask you which other centers you have visited or plan to visit. They may volunteer information about other places you have been to, or plan to see. You may find that the director at one center has been the director or head teacher at another center. Directors and teachers can give you interesting information about other centers. Do be selective in evaluating what they tell you. If they talk to you about a "competing" center, or a place they formerly held a job, they may be overly critical. But, if her center is not logistically right for you, then a center director may be helpful in telling you where else to look.

Visiting Day Care Centers

Make observations about a day care center's physical environment as you drive or walk up to it. Is the outside well kept and neat? Does it look more institutional or homelike? Is there a convenient place to drop off your child? Is there outdoor play space? Are fences, gates, and doors between the day care center and the sidewalk, road, or parking lot secured? (I remember one center I don't like, and the first time I visited it. Before I made it through their lovely, carved-wood, double front doors, I found myself chasing down a three-year-old who had appeared, unaccompanied, from inside. When I went into the fern-filled lobby, the receptionist thanked me for retrieving him, but showed no particular alarm or even awareness that he had escaped.)

When you go inside a center, you will find yourself either in a reception area or right in a classroom. Many directors prefer to give you an introduction to their programs in their offices and then let you observe. Others take a less active approach: the head teacher may greet you from a distance, "Hi! Come on in and look around. Let me know if you have any questions." Sometimes, you'll be invited to let your child participate for a while, and then ask questions later. If you arrive during a group activity time, such as "sharing" or singing, you'll probably have to wait until the teacher can disengage herself before you can ask questions.

In a day care center, the observing will be more important than the interviewing. You will want to see how the adults function as a team, and how the children interact with them. Interviewing may be the best way to find out about a single caregiver, but observing will tell you more than asking any one teacher about herself or other teachers. While you observe, you may want to try chatting with a teacher or two, as they come in contact with your child. Try to get a feeling about how much they like their job and the children.

The interview portion of your day care center visits should be comparatively brief. The questions should pertain to *what* the center does for children. Your observations will tell you *how well* they do the things they do. Here are a few additional open-ended questions to ask when you visit a day care center:

- What is your center's philosophy in caring for children? Or, What do you feel is most important in caring for children (the age of your child)? Answers should include things such as "emotional well-being," and "learning to learn"; health and safety should go almost without saying.
- Are there any formal instructional components to the program? For example, learning colors, shapes, phonics. Are these taught to age-appropriate groups?
- How do you go about choosing staff? What are your educational requirements of staff? What do you like in a teacher?
- Can you tell me a little about how your program has changed over the past year? Probe for information about staff turnover, and changes initiated by parents.
- Do you have parent contracts? (Get a copy.) Do you have a parent board? Parent meetings?
- Review the fees. Make sure you know the right cost for the age of your child, including any transportation fees, meals, extended day care, overtime fees, late-payment fees, deposits and advance payments. Find out when payments are due and to whom.

If you begin your interview in the director's office, your next move should be into one of the classrooms. A director who simply shows you the rooms and points out aspects of the physical facility is probably trying to avoid having you take a hard look at the program.

Find a room that has children the age of your child. Put your child down and let him do what he wants. Sit back and observe.

Sit on the floor so you'll be as inconspicuous and unobtrusive as possible. When observing, don't stare directly at anyone. Instead, glance around periodically so that the objects of your observation will not feel unnecessarily self-conscious.

There are two methods of systematic observation that you may want to try. The first involves person-focused observation. Pick one child in the room to follow. Watch only that child and those he comes in contact with for at least five minutes. See how he spends his time. How much of the time is he actively playing? How often is he uninvolved? How frequently does he come in contact with caregivers? How long do these contacts last? What are they like? Playful? Instructional? Routine? Expressive or unemotional? If you have time, pick another child who seems somewhat different and repeat the procedure. By watching one child constantly, you'll come close to getting an unbiased estimate of how your child might use her time in that day care center. You'll be amazed at what a different impression you can get if you just follow one child.

Then pick one teacher to watch. How much time does she spend with children versus in preparatory or administrative tasks? Does she do more play and instruction than management? Does her face look relaxed, tense or bland? Does she reflect an enjoyment about the way children do things? How long does she spend with each child? Does she cut off interactions before the child seems to have had "enough" of her? Is she able to understand what children want? Ideally, if you have enough time, you might want to repeat this observation for each teacher in the room. It will help you become familiar with their individual styles as well as give you information about how competent they are in handling children.

The second type of systematic observation you can do in a day care center classroom is called event-sampling. When you event-sample, you keep your eyes open for certain activities and events, such as fighting over toys, aggression, and crying. How long does it take teachers to react to and intervene in each incident? Do their approaches to problems demonstrate creative understanding of what each child involved in the conflict is experiencing? For example, one of my all-time favorite caregivers handled aggression in a thoughtful, unique way: most caregivers break up a fight by first reprimanding the aggressor, and later, comforting the victim. This woman, Angelina, would stop the fight, and comfort the victim first, then catch up with the aggressor, who always knew his "just deserts" would be forthcoming. Her method took the reward of immediate attention away from the bad kid and gave it to the good kid. It also gave the bad kid some time to reflect and feel remorse, before facing up to his scolding. This caregiver had created her own way to handle difficult situations, and demonstrated that she understood how children were affected by her actions.

Looking at how stressful events are handled will tell you a great deal about the quality of a center's care. After you have finished observing specific people and events, there are a few other criteria you may want to include in your rating of a center.

How did your child do? Did she join in? Did she seem at ease? Do you think she would like to come back and "visit" again? If she's old enough, ask her.

Think about the overall atmosphere of the center and the feelings that you had about it. Here are some descriptive dimensions of day care center programs that have been examined by one Southern California research team. These "poles" do not represent good versus bad features; rather, they show different kinds of experiences that children can have when in day care. Were the children

- emotionally expressive or learning to control feelings?
- being cared for or being independent?
- acting individually or being part of a group?
- in adult or peer relationships?
- active or inactive?
- entertaining themselves or learning to obey rules about doing things?
- running, jumping, tumbling, or writing, reading, making music?
- having free time or doing things when they're told?
- following a routine or doing new things?
- experiencing nature or learning about man-made things?

Most centers will have a blend that provides children with all kinds of learning opportunities. Thinking of day care centers in terms of these dimensions is one way for you to compare them. Variety is important, but equally important is whether what you saw is what you want.

Once you've seen three to five day care centers, you may have a good idea of what's out there and what you want. You may get an opening where you want it, and right away. More likely, you'll put your child's name on three or four waiting lists and wait. All you can do is hope that the timing will work out.

If a sizable amount of time elapses between when you've seen the center and when you are notified of an opening, you may want to visit again before making a final decision. A revisit would be especially important if your child is now old enough for a different room than the one you originally visited.

When you accept an opening, call back the other centers you are wait-listed at and let them know your decision. You could drop the director a note in the mail, rather than calling, if you're more comfortable with that. It is important to take your name off the waiting list so that the center and other parents can better estimate their chances for an opening.

If you have decided against a center because of some feature of the program or because of a particular teacher, you'll be providing the director with valuable information by giving her those reasons. If the location, cost, or hours were just not right, then say so.

When you have completed the steps in this chapter, you will have selected a day care arrangement using the best information available to you. The day care battle is only partly won. Next you must finalize arrangements, help your child and yourself adjust to the new situation, and develop means of keeping your day care arrangement running smoothly.

Chapter 6

Making Day Care Arrangements

STABILITY IN A DAY CARE arrangement can be so important to a child's developing sense of continuity of events. The parent necessarily lacks the child's view on continuity in the day care arrangement, because the parent is not there all day, and the child is. The only thing that changes for a parent when a day care arrangement changes, is that there is a new face to greet each morning and afternoon. The child, on the other hand, is having his whole day restructured. A University of Minnesota study of day care in the first year of life reported that inconsistency in caregivers may contribute to a child's anxious attachment to his parents.

Many families change day care amazingly often. The parental side of the story is that things did not work out as expected. (Almost always, these are parents who chose the first day care arrangement they could find.) The caregiver's side of the story is that she can't imagine what it was that these parents were expecting. The kid's side of the story is that he has become more removed, less involved, and less affectionate with each successive caregiver. Often, parents will drop a day care arrangement for quite inconsequential reasons. Often, if more had been stated about mutual expectations before ever starting the arrangement, it would probably have been able to continue.

The most common reason for changing day care arrangements is disagreements between parents and caregivers. It is essential that you agree, up front, on what you expect to receive for your money. Some parents may feel that it is onerous to deal in a businesslike way with someone who, in a sense, is going to be their child's surrogate parent. But it is necessary.

Some parents believe that if they move their child from one care arrangement to another that might be better in some way, they have netted a profit. This is not necessarily the case. What are the effects of changing day care arrangements frequently? This question is not answerable in absolute terms. But I would rather see a child in one mediocre arrangement for a year and a half, than in three excellent ones for six months each. Children just can't take full advantage of the resources available to them in a good day care arrangement if they are constantly being shuffled around and required to readjust.

The research on day care has made only some initial inroads in helping us understand how frequent changes of day care arrangements affect children. It has been difficult to study the effects of unstable day care because children who change day care frequently, often also experience other family changes, such as new siblings, divorce, and remarriage of parents. There is good reason to believe that frequent changes of day care arrangements can confuse a child, make him less secure, and perhaps less trusting and responsive in new situations. Some children will be more affected by changing day care arrangements than will other children. Since we know that children are sensitive to changes in their routines, it's a good idea to anticipate problems that might bring an otherwise satisfactory day care arrangement to an end.

THE DAY CARE CONTRACT

Many day care centers and some family day care homes use standard contracts that specify cost, pick-up and delivery schedules, late fees, vacation and sick-child policy. The contracts are not so much legal documents as they are explicit agreements between parents and caregivers. You should seriously consider using a day care contract.

Day care contracts are most useful for confronting practical issues. They can also be used to specify your expectations for main features of the care your child will receive. For example, a contract might include a sentence about acceptable methods of discipline.

Caregivers who haven't had any prior experience with contracts may be a little apprehensive at first. The prospect of any contract is likely to be somewhat intimidating. (If you are a lawyer, your caregiver may be all the more intimidated.) A contract is really just a tool that can help people communicate with one another. Once the contract is negotiated and signed, it will be behind you. It will give you a solid foundation for your working relationship with your caregiver or day care center. It also reinforces the formal professional responsibilities the role of care provider entails.

If you explain how your day care contract will protect and respect the caregiver's rights, as well as yours, the caregiver should agree to negotiate it with you. You should also explain to caregivers that you don't really intend this to be a legal contract, but rather a formal means of understanding one another.

Most day care centers write their own agreements with parents. You may want to ask the director about adding to the contract if there are important topics that you feel are not covered well enough. The sample contracts later in this chapter give examples of issues you may want to include in your contract.

Family day care mothers who are sponsored through a network or belong to an association may have their own contracts. The nicest family day care contracts are written in the first person singular by the day care mother, to the parents. In certain areas, licensed day care mothers will have been provided with sample contracts by their licensing agency or local information and referral agencies.

It will be up to you to provide a contract if you hire an in-home provider. Contracts with in-home caregivers are, perhaps, more important than in other forms of day care, since you will be paying for the luxury of having a great deal of control over what the caregiver will and will not do while she is in your home.

In the sample contracts given later in this chapter, you will be provided with a list of items to include. The items on the list include: practical considerations, quality assurances, and provisions for change over time. Depending on your situation, some of the options may not seem worth choosing (i.e., too unlikely). Each option on the list is included because it has been a *real* reason that some *real* day care arrangement broke up. (If marriages can fail because one spouse didn't like the way the other squeezed toothpaste and strained orange juice, it shouldn't be surprising that a day care arrangement fails because a day care mother repeatedly observed an "emergency" candy bar at the bottom of a diaper bag.)

The truth of the matter is this: by including provisions for regulating both important and trivial matters in a day care contract, you set the tone for being able to talk about these topics and others that come up. As in the case of the toothpaste and orange juice family, as well as the candy-bar day care mother, the details were just the tip of the iceberg. The trivial issues that become the battleground for terminating the relationship are just symptomatic expressions of deep-seated inability to communicate.

For example, Janine, the day care mother who resented Joshua's daily candy bar, really saw the candy as just one more sign of his mother's overindulgent attitude toward him. She felt Joshua's hyperactive behavior was caused by his lack of restrictions at home. What *really* had horrified her was the day Phyllis, Joshua's mother, had said, "If he doesn't want the kind of lunch you make him, just give him this candy instead." An insult to her cooking and her sensibilities in one blow! After several more potshots like that, it became impossible for Janine and Phyllis to sit down and discuss any real issues, such as getting Joshua on a schedule of eating wholesome meals. The loser in this case was Joshua, because Janine was really great with kids, and his new arrangement just wasn't as good.

Day care contracts help you avoid taking the "School of Hard Knocks" course on finding day care. I have no doubt that if your first day care arrangement broke up because you felt your housekeeper didn't spend enough time out-of-doors with your kids, you would remember to include a question on spending time outside when you interviewed a second round of housekeepers. The purpose of the day care contract is to get things right the first time around. Even if you opt not to have a written day care contract, the issues addressed in the contracts that follow should constitute topics of verbal agreement between you and your caregiver(s).

Medical Consent and Health History

Whenever you start a day care arrangement, it is a good idea to have a medical consent form as part of your agreement or contract. You should also provide the caregiver or center with information on your whereabouts during the day. These pieces of information are essential. Many parents feel more than a little discomfort when they sign away their responsibility in a potential emergency. You should realize that some hospital emergency rooms, clinics, or physicians may be reluctant or even legally unable to administer care in the absence of an authorized consent for treatment. In the cases of poisoning, severe bleeding, or loss of consciousness, for example, immediate treatment may be necessary to save a child's life. Young children climb, crawl, and orally explore. Their level of activity increases the likelihood that something will happen to them. No matter how good and well supervised a day care arrangement is, accidents can happen. It is important to sign a medical release form so your child's caregiver can get him care if and when he needs it.

You will have to write your own release for an in-home or family day care arrangement. Most day care centers are required by law to have them on file. For example:

- I, (parent), authorize (caregiver/center) to seek emergency medical care for (child) when I cannot be reached by telephone, or in a life-threatening situation.
  Signature————————————————————————
  Date————————————

- (Parents) release medical custody of (child). If possible, seek medical attention from (doctor's name) or (hospital) in case of a medical emergency.
  Signature————————————————————————
  Date————————————

In addition to a medical treatment consent form, day care centers and some day care networks will require you to provide them with a record of your child's health history. This allows them to determine immunity or susceptibility to particular diseases, as well as the adequacy of the vaccination series the child has received. Here's a list of the immunizations and diseases they are likely to need to include in a medical history. (You might as well make a list of these and the dates they occurred, ahead of time. It will save you last-minute hassle and running around to collect the information from your pediatrician or clinic.)

- Immunizations — dates of the following: DPT first, DPT second, DPT third, booster first, booster second, poliomyelitis, mumps, rubella, measles. (Children younger than two will not yet have completed the required series.)
- Illness history — age at onset of the following: chickenpox, asthma, rheumatic fever, ten-day measles, hay fever, diabetes, three-day "German measles" (rubella), epilepsy, whooping cough, mumps, poliomyelitis.
- Current medications.

The health history you may be asked to provide may include other questions as well. Usually these questions screen for physical abnormalities and gross emotional disturbances. Some states require parents to fill in forms about the child's normal daily behavior. These questions are supposed to help caregivers better understand the child's abilities and background.

When you meet with the caregiver or center director to draw up a contract or otherwise finalize arrangements, it will be a good time to fill out the health history also. It will be awkward and uncomfortable to do this on the first day of an arrangement, when you will really be needing to pay full attention to your child.

Parent Information Card

One important thing your caregiver or center will need is a parent information card. This card should provide your home and work telephone numbers, your spouse's name and work telephone, your home address, and where you can be reached at different hours of the day if you move around. Also include the name of your child's physician and his phone number and address. Including the phone numbers of the local poison-control center, emergency room, and ambulance service can't hurt either. If your caregiver is not primarily English-speaking, make sure she can read what you have given her. You might suggest that she translate it into her first language.

Contracts for In-home Caregivers

The Swifts live in a nice section of upper Manhattan. Elmira Stands has agreed to be their housekeeper. Geoffrey and Louise Swift work full time and have an eighteen-month-old, Peter, and an eight-year-old, Anna. Here's a contract that they've tailored for themselves.

In-Home Day Care Contract

This is an agreement between Geoffrey and Louise Swift and Elmira Stands to provide child care for Peter and Anna Swift.

HOURS AND SALARY

- The hours you are to be at our house are 8:30 A.M. to 6:00 P.M.
- The days of the week you will work are Monday through Friday.
- You will be paid $180 per week minus what we withhold for income tax, FICA, and FUTA.
- Every six months, either of us may opt for a pay increase, not to exceed 5 percent of the initial salary.
- Overtime pay will be $4.00 per hour.
- Nighttime babysitting will pay $3.00 per hour.
- We have the option of withholding $2.50 from your salary for every fifteen minutes you are delayed in the morning.
- If you must miss work because you're sick, you will try to get a substitute or call the night before. You will be paid only for days you actually work.
- You will be paid every Friday at the end of the day.

HOUSEHOLD DUTIES

In addition to caring for Peter and Anna, which will be your most important job and first responsibility, you agree to do these other household duties:

- Cleaning up the kitchen, including cleaning up from any meals when you weren't here.
- Laundry for everyone in the family.
- Vacuuming, mopping, sweeping, and dusting.
- Weekly linen changes and bathroom cleanup.
- Watering the terrace and household plants.
- Grocery shopping as necessary (I will provide grocery lists).
- Cooking Peter's breakfast and lunch, and preparing the family's dinner for 6:30 each evening.
- Transporting Peter and Anna to and from gymnastics twice a week in the afternoon.

HOUSEHOLD RULES

- It is fine to bring along your youngest son.
- Preferably, other friends of yours should not visit, or visit only briefly, during your working hours.
- You will answer the phone and take messages as necessary.
- You may make any meals you want for yourself from the normal family grocery supplies.
- Anna has our permission to play in the building or next door after school, but she must check in with you first, and be back by 6:00.
- It is OK to use the stereo and TV. The TV should be on only for selected children's shows or when Peter is napping.

DO'S AND DON'TS FOR PETER

We both understand that it is not possible to specify exactly how you and Peter will spend your time together. Largely, it is up to your good judgment. These are a few guidelines:

- Peter can only have his pacifier and bottle at nap and bedtimes.
- Peter must eat a good portion of his meals to get dessert.
- He is not allowed to have gum or candy.
- He must have his vitamins at breakfast.
- When he starts to do something very dangerous, it's OK to slap his hand; otherwise no spanking of any kind.
- If he has defied you he must go to his room for a short "time-out."
- He must have a nap or at least a rest in bed every day after lunch.
- In nice weather, Peter should go out for walks, to the park, or shopping sometime each day.
- Some days I may arrange for you to take Peter to a friend's apartment to play.

GRIEVANCES

If you have any problems with Peter or Anna, we should both feel free to talk about them as soon as they happen. Here are things we both can do if there are any problems:

- The first week of your employment is a trial period. If taking care of Peter is not what you expected, or if things between you and Peter are not what we expected, then either one of us is free to end the arrangement at that time.
- If problems arise during the day, and they can't wait until the afternoon to be solved, you should call me at work. In a medical emergency you should call Dr. Howard or the Mid-Town Hospital Emergency Room first.
- We will reserve 6:00 to 6:30 on Friday as a time for us to talk about the past week, and the coming week, and any difficulties that have arisen.

The best way to come up with the specifics of a contract like this is to keep a running list of your concerns and your child's habits and activities. Such a contract requires care and forethought.

In-home Share Care Arrangement

The in-home day care contract we've just seen gives examples of how you can control a child care arrangement in your own home. If you opt for the share-care variety of in-home care, and plan to share a caregiver with one or more other families, you might proceed a bit differently. First of all, many of the items from the contract list should be negotiated jointly by the families sharing care prior to finding a caregiver. In this sense, the day-care contract will be like an agreement to form a partnership. The partners need to specify to one another, as well as to an employee, what the obligations of each party will be.

Ellen, Evelyn, Marie, and their husbands live in the same townhouse complex in Houston, Texas. Ellen's eight-month-old, Max, is currently in a family day care arrangement rather far from Ellen's home and work. Her friend Evelyn has a six-month-old, Jonah, and is about to return to work. Marie is a neighbor of Evelyn's and is six months pregnant. She will have only a twelve-week maternity leave from her job. Ellen and Evelyn decide to look for a caregiver they can share. Marie decided to look with them so that she can have day care planned for six months from now when she'll have had her baby and will need to return to work. Here's what they agreed upon in advance:

Share-Care Day Care Contract
THE PARTNERSHIP

We agree to form a partnership to find, hire, and pay a joint caregiver for our children.

- We will jointly hire a caregiver who will be paid weekly, by each of us separately.
- She will be hired only to provide child care, no housework, although she'll provide meals for the children and clean up after them as necessary.
- Each family will supply its own baby equipment as needed.

- We will rotate our homes as the day care center; Evelyn's house first since day care will be newest to Jonah; Ellen's next; Marie's when she's ready to join in.
- The only additional duty of the "house" mother is to stay each morning until the caregiver arrives, and to cover for late pickups.
- We agree to share days staying with all three children if the caregiver is absent.
- We will change houses every three or four months.
- The caregiver will have national holidays off and one mutually agreed-upon week per year as paid vacation.
- A sick child is one who has a fever over 100 degrees, or is vomiting, or has a contagious disease (not colds, earaches, and so on). Sick children will be kept home until the symptoms disappear.

Shortly after preparing the partnership papers, Ellen, Evelyn, and Marie began interviewing caregivers. At least two of them were present at each interview. Loreli was the fourth woman with whom they all spoke. Loreli had worked in a day care center two years earlier and had a Child Development Associate credential. She had just burned out as a receptionist, and wanted to go back to working with children. She felt this job would complement the early education classes she was taking in the evening.

This section of the contract, and the sections that follow, are negotiated with the caregiver.

HOURS AND SALARY

This is an agreement between our partnership and Loreli Hoffswagner. You should consider each of us, equally, to be your employer, even though you will only be in one of our homes at a time.

- The hours you work will be 8:00 A.M. to 5:00 P.M.
- The days of the week you will work are Monday through Friday.
- You will be paid a total of $180 per week, in three separate sums, one from each family ($120 per week until there are three children).
- You will be responsible for your own taxes and Social Security.

- Every six months, either you or we may opt for a pay increase, not to exceed 10 percent of the initial salary.
- We have the option of withholding $5.00 from your salary for every half-hour you are late each morning.
- You will be paid every Friday afternoon.

HOUSEHOLD RULES

- The children are allowed to be in the kitchen, family room, and their own bedrooms.
- You have no housework expected of you, except preparing and cleaning up from the children's meals.
- Each mother will provide you with her own child's food and baby supplies.
- We request that you avoid visits and phone calls from friends during your working hours.
- The children should only be allowed in the yard if you are with them, never alone.
- Please watch TV only if all the children are napping.

DO'S AND DON'TS FOR THE CHILDREN

We have selected you because we feel you will do the right things for our children. In addition, we are providing you with some guidelines so you'll know where we stand on some issues we feel are important:
- Please try and follow each mother's directives for her child.
- If the needs of different children conflict, speak to their mothers as soon as there's a problem.
- In nice weather, take the children outside for part of the day.
- Try to help the children play with each other.
- Check with each mother about how her child should be disciplined and when.

GRIEVANCES

If problems arise with any of the children, or between you and one of us, we want you to feel free to discuss matters with us individually or as a group. Here are some ways to handle mutual problems:

- The first week is a trial period for all of us. If any of us, or if you, find that this arrangement is not working out as expected, any one parent is free to withdraw, or you will be free to look for another job.
- A personal problem with one mother or one child can be handled by calling any of us after child care hours.
- We will reserve Thursday afternoons, from 5:30 on, for you and all of us to discuss the week.
- Please give us four weeks' notice if you plan to terminate your job.

Contracts for Family Day Care Mothers

The purpose of a day care contract with a family day care mother is slightly different from that of a contract with an in-home caregiver. You are entering your child in an already existing routine at the day care mother's home. It is a routine that has evolved to her satisfaction and to the satisfaction of parents who found her before you did. Therefore, your contract with a family day care mother will be more oriented toward the understanding of practical issues. If your day care mother has a contract she already uses, you'll probably find that most of the items on it have to do with cost, sick care, vacations, and so on.

The whole reason you would use a day care contract is to insure a smooth, long-running day care arrangement. Family day care arrangements are, statistically, the least stable form of day care. (This is often thought to be more strongly related to the transitional characteristics of families using family day care rather than to the arrangements themselves.) You will demonstrate your expectation for a long-term day care arrangement when you suggest having a contract. This can be an important psychological edge in developing a commitment from a day care mother who, in the past, has had to deal with flaky families who vacillate concerning what they expect. Below are sample day care contracts for two families with rather different needs in a family day care arrangement.

Frances Lombardi is the single mother of Todd, a shy, untalkative, two-and-a-half-year-old boy. Frances feels that he has failed to "blossom" much in the center where he's been since he was eight months old. She wants to try family day care, where she feels he'll get more one-to-one attention. Her problem is that she needs drop-in hours because she is a relief nurse. Finally, she meets Barbara Wheller, a forty-year-old day care mother, who sticks close to home because of her own four children, four to fourteen years old. Here's Frances's contract with Barbara.

Family Day Care Contract

This is an agreement between Frances Lombardi, parent, and Barbara Wheller, day care mother, for the care of Todd Lombardi.

- Barbara agrees to be available for Frances, 6:00 A.M.–12:00 noon, any day of the week.
- Todd will attend day care between 30 and 40 hours per week.
- Frances will "buy" from Barbara a minimum of 30 hours of care per week, even if Todd comes for fewer hours.
- The hourly fee will depend on the time of day: 6:00 A.M.–5:00 P.M., $1.75 per hour; 5:00 P.M.–9:00 P.M., $1.50 per hour; 9:00 P.M.–midnight, $1.00 per hour. All night, over night will cost $1.00 per hour. (All fees will be $.50 per hour more on Saturdays and Sundays.)
- Payment will be on the last day of each week.
- Barbara agrees to take Todd even if he is sick.
- Barbara will provide a substitute for regular hours only, on days she is sick or on vacation.
- Barbara will give Frances a weekly, itemized list of money spent on Todd's food and disposable diapers, to be added to each week's fees.
- Frances will provide Barbara with complete changes of clothes for all weather.
- Frances will call Barbara at least one hour in advance of bringing Todd, and one hour prior to pickup.
- If Barbara takes Todd out, Frances will pay for any additional time he spends with Barbara until they return home and Todd can be picked up.

Behavior Guidelines

Here is a list of "growing-up" behaviors to work on with Todd. Frances asks that Barbara work on these with Todd, and in return gives Barbara permission to train, discipline, and teach Todd in the way she feels is best.
- Playing more with other children.
- Speaking when spoken to.
- Toilet-training.
- Sharing.

Another family, the Berks, who live in Lawrence, Kansas, have looked for, and found, a family day care home that resembles a small school; it has two caregivers and ten children. Before starting their daughter Arla, Cora and Allan Berk want to write a contract that not only spells out practical issues, but also assures them that the rather unique schoollike character of this day care home will remain a part of the picture. Some of the items in their contracts were taken from the one their caregivers often use. The Berks edited it, and added their own concerns to those of the caregivers.

Family Day Care Contract

This is an agreement between Jo Ellen McFadden and Jean Britton, and Cora and Allan Berk to provide family day care for their daughter, Arla Berk.

Hours and Salary

- Day care will be provided 9:00 A.M. to 5:00 P.M., Monday through Friday.
- Weekly fee is $60 per week.
- Weekly group trips will be added to weekly costs as necessary.
- Extended day care, before 9:00 A.M. or after 6:00 P.M., will be charged at a rate of $2.00 per hour, by 15 minute intervals.
- Days missed will be paid in full.

THE PROGRAM

- The fees include a morning preschool program and afternoon free-play period.
- Caregiver-child ratio will not exceed 1:5.
- All children will be two years old or older.
- The Berks will provide a box lunch; Jo Ellen and Jean will provide morning and afternoon snack.
- The fee includes once-weekly group lessons in the day care home from a music teacher and an art teacher.
- Any religious content to the program, celebration of holidays, and so forth, will be discussed with parents in advance.

DO'S AND DON'TS

- If Arla has a cold, fever, or diarrhea, she cannot come to day care.
- If Arla is going to miss a day, Cora and Allan will call the night before.
- Arla will not bring personal playthings from home.
- All children nap or rest between 12:00 and 1:30.

Contracts with Day Care Centers

Contracts with day care centers are written by the centers themselves. You may ask for the addition of items not in the standard contract, but it probably won't have a substantial impact on the type of care your child receives. Day care center contracts are prepared to outline fees and hours of operations, and to meet licensing, health, and safety requirements. Most day care centers have a monthly fee schedule. Weekly payments would just be too much paperwork for them to handle. Generally, day care center contracts are quite bare-bones explanations of how things are done.

If you have questions about how certain situations would be handled, ask for a verbal confirmation about how the staff would proceed. Make sure you understand the best route for addressing issues with caregivers at different levels in the staff structure.

Public and private nonprofit centers will offer similar contracts. Parent cooperative centers may have more involved contracts that spell out what is expected of the parent, as well as services to the child.

Here are two sample contracts with day care centers. The first one is between a family that is eligible for a day care subsidy and is going to use a publicly funded day care center with a morning Head Start program. The second one is between a family and a parent cooperative association that is just starting a day care center.

The first family, the Luces, have a daughter, Patricia, who is three. Her father, Anthony, is finishing his last year of college in Ann Arbor, Michigan, and her mother, Kathleen, works as a secretary. After ten months on the waiting list for Evergreen Hall Child Development Center, they are informed of an opening. This is the standard contract they signed with the center.

Evergreen Hall Child Development Center
Parent Agreement

Anthony and Kathleen Luce, parents of Patricia Luce, agree to the following:
- Payment of monthly fees in advance, due by the 9th of each month; parents will be credited for days missed.
- An initial $25 deposit is required of each family.
- Children may be dropped off between 6:30 A.M. and 8:45 A.M.
- Pickup between 4:00 P.M. and 6:45 P.M.
- Parents must sign the child in and out of the center each day. (Sign-up sheets are in the front office.)
- Parents arriving after 6:45 P.M. will pay a $2.00 per 15 minutes overtime charge.
- Parents receiving subsidy (paying on a sliding scale) are required to notify the center of a change in income.
- The daily program will include:
  8:00 A.M.   Hot breakfast (provided).
  9:00 A.M.–noon   Head Start for 2–5 year olds.
  Noon–2:30 or 3:00 P.M.   Hot lunch (provided) plus nap/rest-time.

3:00 P.M. on   Supervised indoor and outdoor recreation time.
- The center will be closed on all school holidays.

The second family, the Hollenbecks, had looked for a day care center unsuccessfully. When they were about to give up the idea of Vicky returning to work just yet, they heard that a group of parents affiliated with their church wanted to start a cooperative day care center. Several of these families were presently participating in a home-based, rotating "babysitting" co-op. Many of the children in the co-op were now two to three years old and the parents had decided to try to formalize their group and run a day care center with their children plus some others. Vicky had planned not to work full time, and the idea of spending some of her time with her twins, Dale and Dawn, in a group setting appealed to her. She had found that the special interdependence of her twins on one another made it difficult for them to relate to other three-year-olds. By volunteering time to the co-op center, she felt she would be there to aid her children's adjustment to peers. Her husband, Owen, favored the idea too. The fathers of the co-op association planned to spend one weekend a month building playground equipment and classroom furniture for the center. Owen liked the idea of making a concrete contribution to the place his children would be all day, since he didn't have time to be there himself.

This is the agreement that the Hollenbecks and other families signed as they joined the co-op day care center.

Springfield Valley Day Care Cooperative Association

THE CO-OP

- Payment for day care will be made in service hours and in parent fees.
- All payments will be made to the co-op fund and be used for head-teacher salary, rent, and classroom and building materials.

- Parent fees will be $60 per week per child; $110 per week for two children.
- Ten volunteer hours per week per family per child are required.
- Extra fees: September to May all children will be taken once a week to Kinder-Gym. June to August all children will be taken once a week to YMCA "Minnows" swim class. Parents will be notified of these fees.
- Volunteer time includes classroom time, bookkeeping time, grocery shopping, and building time on weekends.
- Additional volunteer hours will be credited to parent fees at $2.00 per hour.
- All parents are asked to attend monthly parent board meetings, held the last Wednesday of each month at 8:00 P.M. The board meetings will include a review of finances, building projects, and discussion time for hearing parent suggestions and grievances about the program.

THE PROGRAM

- Class size will not exceed 15.
- Caregiver to child ratio will not exceed 1:5.
- One head teacher/director will be hired.
- The teacher salary, raises, and contract will be voted on by the parent board.
- Other classroom assistance will come from parents.
- The teacher will supervise parents in the classroom and assign responsibilities.
- Parent suggestions to the teacher will be reserved for board meetings.
- The program will be unstructured. Teachers will be there to facilitate the activities of children rather than to create them.
- Families will send box lunches and snacks, mats and blankets for naps.
- Hours of operation will be 8:30 A.M.–5:30 P.M.
- Full- or half-day children only.
- The center will try to arrange sick-child care in the home of one of the participating families.

You Will Get What You Ask For

You know day care contracts are important so that both parties involved understand what is expected of them. They are one way you can assure the quality of your child's care.

In the United States, we have come to expect the government to regulate the quality of our schools, our food, our medical care, et cetera. We don't worry too much about these things because we know there is some bureaucrat in Washington, D.C., generating reams of regulations about what type of preservatives can be put in our bacon, how much of it we can eat and not get cancer, and so on.

We do need to worry about the quality of day care. The federal government has declined to participate in regulating child care. This means that it is up to individual states to regulate day care. A couple of states have no day care regulations. Other states essentially regulate only health and safety (i.e., no exposed electrical wires, no peeling lead paint), but not program characteristics. The suggestion that day care regulation be instituted in one state (Florida), where there have been no day care laws, has met stiff opposition. The political climate for legislation benefiting children is not favorable.

Newly drafted federal regulations for day care, which were supposed to go into effect around July 1981, were killed by "New Federalism" politicians trying to look as though they were saving your tax dollars and giving government back to the "little guy." Some states are likely to jump on this bandwagon, ridding themselves of what regulations they now have. (After all, the money-saving legislators will agree, if Florida can make it without day care regulations, why can't we?) That this backward movement in day care regulation will persist becomes increasingly likely now that the states are being asked to provide regulatory services for which the federal government used to be responsible.

So, it is up to parents to control the quality of day care. By stating what you want, verbally or in a contract, you make it clear that you expect good-quality services for your money.

Day care is no longer the unfortunate alternative for families that "have to" leave their children to work, in order to survive. Whether you go to school, take time for yourself, or work because you want to, have to, or both, you deserve good-quality care. It is time for families to stop accepting poor-quality care as part of some imagined, inevitable misfortune.

Now that you know about how day care may affect children, you can see that it is important to avoid conditions in day care that may have a negative impact on your child's development. Therefore, it is important to use this information, and make it work for you. It's up to you to create a day care environment that offers your child potential benefits. Insist on individual attention, on small groups, on prompt responses to your child's needs. You should not assume that there is any Big Brother out there, regulating things, insisting on it for you.

Once your day care arrangement is made, it's much more difficult to change things than if you draw a hard line from the start. If you ask for a quality assurance in your day care contract that no parent has asked for before, don't be put off. You will be serving your own ends, by getting what you want for your child. You will also be serving a common good by letting day care providers know that you, as a parent, know what is best, and the best is what you expect.

Helping Your Child and Yourself Adjust to Day Care

IT'S TIME FOR the first day of your newly planned child care arrangement. What do you want to know about how this day will be? How can you help it to be a good experience for your child? For yourself?

This chapter will address the gnawing apprehensions that some mothers have about returning to work, what soothes those feelings, how separation affects children of different ages, and what parents can do to minimize departure protest and separation anxiety.

HOW MOTHERS FEEL ABOUT LEAVING THEIR CHILDREN

There has been a whole body of research on the effects of maternal employment. Some researchers have been interested in how family earnings or sex roles change when a mother works. Other research has examined the effects of maternal employment on the woman's satisfaction as a mother.

What is the relationship between a mother's satisfaction with her status as a worker and her feelings about being a mother? This complex issue has only begun to be addressed. Among the earliest studies of maternal employment and satisfaction with child-rearing was one made in 1962, comparing mothers who did and did not work, and satisfaction with work or nonwork roles. The mothers who were not satisfied with their roles (that is, the mothers who worked and wished they didn't, and the ones who didn't and wished they did) were less satisfied with their effectiveness as mothers than the women who were doing what they wanted to be doing, regardless of whether that meant working or staying at home.

A recent Ohio State University study showed that mothers who worked, while believing that they were the only ones really qualified to care for their babies, had babies who reacted more negatively than babies of mothers who did not feel so irreplaceable. Further, the greater the extent to which a mother feels irreplaceable for her baby, the greater her apprehension about nonmaternal care; the more intense her sense that her baby is attached to her, the greater the feeling that the very young baby does discriminate her from other caregivers, and the more heightened the perception of the baby's stress at separation from her. In fact, the babies of mothers who feel this do demonstrate more stress at separation.

So what do you do? Not go back to work? Never leave your baby? No. You use your awareness of the influence of your attitudes upon your child's adjustment to make things easier for yourself, and hence for your child. If you and your child prepare emotionally to begin day care, you will minimize adjustment reactions. A mother's attitude or satisfaction with working may have a lot to do with a child's resources when it comes to adjusting to day care. Children take cues about how to behave and feel from parents. A somewhat negative parental attitude toward working and/or leaving the child can be communicated to a child: "It's a terrible thing to have Mommy gone." Even very young children can sense the anxiety of either parent as they talk about using day care or the mother's going back to work. If the parents have different ideas about whether the mother should be in or out of the house, a child will sense the parental ambivalence. As parents, you should resolve these issues together, without having the child present; then you can present your child with a solid decision to which you have committed yourselves.

Here are two contrasting cases: first, a mother who wished she worked, but didn't; second, a mother who worked and wished she didn't.

The first mother-and-child pair, Kerry and Jeff Carlisle, exemplify what happens when a mother stays home and doesn't want to. Kerry had been a successful administrator at a large utility company. After Jeff's birth, her husband and family coerced her into the "luxury" of staying home and raising her child herself. Kerry had too much energy, and was constantly redecorating, cleaning, and hanging onto phone calls and lunchtime visits home by her husband — her link to the "real world," as she explained it. She saw Jeff as much less interesting company than an office full of co-workers. Jeff, a rather difficult, overactive one-year-old, clearly reflected Kerry's desire to be at work. He was often contrary and belligerent, just as she was impatient with him. He was uncuddly and resistant, just as she was often unaffectionate, and resistant to the idea of staying home. I feel that Jeff would have been better off if his mother had worked. Jeff clearly understood that his mother's heart was not at home with him, and he reacted negatively to this. Had Kerry only had a constructive outlet for her energies, and an enhanced sense of self-worth, which formerly her work had given her, she might have been a better mother, though for fewer hours per day.

In contrast, Jan and Jeremy Berger exemplify what happens when a mother who doesn't want to work convinces herself that she should. Jan Berger, a social worker, expressed to me a great deal of discomfort about leaving Jeremy — wondering whether he was really "ready," and so on. She had found a wonderful family day care arrangement, so the quality of care he'd have was not the problem. Jan cried and appeared to be at least as upset as Jeremy during those first few days. During his first six months in family day care, Jeremy's adjustment continued to be rather poor. Although he was a bright boy, the slightest stress would curtail his playing and set him to weeping in a corner. He always eyed visitors suspiciously. With excellent care and understanding, he did come to trust his day care mothers (there were two, a mother-daughter team), but it took much careful drawing out. Jan's attitude about using day care had conveyed to Jeremy that it was a hard thing to have to be separated and that she remained unconvinced that what she was doing was right.

The situations of families like the Carlisles and the Bergers present dilemmas. On one hand, it is quite important to be emotionally honest with your child. But you will need to strike a balance between an emotionally honest recognition of your own apprehensions and the confidence in your decisions that you must exude for your child's sake.

If you are apprehensive, it really does no good to deny it or ignore it. This means of defending yourself against the pain of leaving your child may work in a temporary way. But it is not a healthy means of long-term coping. A good rational self-examination focusing on what makes you feel most uncomfortable about leaving your child should help. Talk about it fully with your spouse or a close friend. Bring your feelings into the open with friends or colleagues who have been through this already. The empathy and understanding of others may really help to assuage your fears and guilt.

Another approach is to voice all concerns about your child's care to his caregivers. Doubtlessly, the most rational parents can and will have lingering questions about what will be happening to their child when they are not there. The only real way to have these questions answered is to see how your child reacts.

Child behavior is often a self-fulfilling prophecy. If you really expect your child to adjust poorly, she probably will. Even very little babies are strong individuals and may surprise you by how easily they can adapt. If you expect your child to adjust successfully to day care, she probably will. But it will take effort on your part.

Your own feeling about separation from your child may depend upon many things. It depends upon how emotionally expressive you are. At first, many mothers do cry or feel like crying. You get used to having your child with you everywhere, then suddenly, you again have "freedom," "one-ness." You may feel as if independence is not what it once was. You may feel empty, alone. These are normal feelings, which abate in intensity as you realize that your child is well cared for in your absence.

Simple things that you do, after you have dropped off your child, may at first make you feel lost, somewhat depressed. For example, you may suddenly realize that you feel strange because you've gotten out of your car without unfolding a stroller or toting a diaper bag.

Nursing mothers have a real physical tie to their babies. If you are nursing, you may feel your milk letting down as your thoughts turn toward your baby, especially as hours of separation accumulate. Just hearing about babies may make you leak.

Some mothers seem to feel it's harder to leave a baby, because a baby is so helpless. Others feel it is harder to leave an older child because a child who can talk can say, "Momma, don't go!" Either way, separation from children can elicit the most powerful emotions. When you begin to use day care, you need to be aware that your own feelings about separation may be stronger than you expected. It's a very natural part of the attachment process. Attachment is a two-way street.

In many families, day care drop-off is primarily the mother's job. In such a situation, the mother bears the parental brunt of separation. If a caregiver comes to your home, separation may be most difficult on the parent who leaves last. If you find the first day or so of leaving your child in day care to be really hard, it may be best for your spouse to do it for a while. That will give you some time to handle your own feelings; bolster yourself, and then address the problem of helping your child with his adjustment.

PREPARING YOUR CHILD FOR THE FIRST DAY

What should you do to prepare your child for the first day of day care? In addition to considering your child's individual needs in a day care arrangement, there are a few stress factors you may need to take into account: separation anxiety, stranger anxiety, and wariness of unfamiliar places. Age will be a major determinant in how you ready your child for the initial days of separation. But remember there is a great deal of normal, individual variation in how stressful children find separations and strangers to be.

Right before you start day care, it might be helpful to gauge just how sensitive to separation your child is, thus making yourself better able to plan the leave-taking process for the first few days of day care. Here's a little experiment to gauge separation anxiety that you can try when someone else (other than the other parent) is at home with you:

- Set your child on the floor and get him playing with some toys and/or with the other person.
- Then explain that you're going into the other room for a moment.
- Leave.

Does your child understand/notice that you've left? How does he react? Does he follow? Does he stay and cry or fret? Repeat the scene, but this time:

- Get your coat or sweater, keys, purse, and act as though you plan to leave the house.
- Again, say good-bye.
- Then go outside for a second.

What reactions does that procedure evoke? Probably you will have gotten more reaction to the second procedure than to the first one. You may expect your child to react similarly during the first day of day care. The reaction may be a bit more heightened if day care also means going to an unfamiliar place. By conducting that little experiment, you have gained some insight into how strong your child's separation anxiety may be when you leave.

You may need to consider a second, equally powerful factor in adjustment reactions: stranger anxiety. Of course, if your child's new caregiver is no stranger to him, stranger anxiety probably will not be much of a concern. However, you should be sensitive to the fact that in your absence, a child may react quite differently to a person he has known only in your presence, even a very familiar figure, such as an aunt or grandmother.

The most logical way to reduce stranger anxiety is to provide your child with opportunities to come to know the unfamiliar person in your reassuring presence. Behavior therapists use a process like this called systematic desensitization. In this case, systematic desensitization involves pairing your presence (the positive stimulus) with the presence of the unfamiliar person (the "aversive" stimulus). Gradually, you increase contact between your child and the caregiver. Through this process the child becomes increasingly (systematically) less sensitive (desensitized) to the fearful aspects of the new person.

Children are often uncomfortable in unfamiliar environments. If you have opted for in-home care, an unfamiliar environment will be one thing that won't contribute to any adjustment reaction your child may have. One study by a North Carolina researcher demonstrated that a strange environment can heighten separation anxiety.

However, some children don't see new environments as strange. Instead, they see them as novel, fun, exciting. For these children, a new place, especially one that is filled with toys and kids, can make them forget they even came with Mom. These children disappear into the scenery the moment you arrive at the day care center or day care home. Such children are easy adapters. They may not even want to say good-bye to you when you go. Do say good-bye, though. Your child might come looking for you in a couple of hours.

There are a few commonsense things you can do if your child does show apprehension of unfamiliar surroundings. First, just being there with him for an initial period will make the place less strange. (The same principle of systematic desensitization that applies to unfamiliar people applies to unfamiliar places, too.) Second, show him around, point out similarities between the place and your home. This will help your child feel more comfortable and well oriented.

TALKING TO YOUR CHILD ABOUT STARTING DAY CARE_____

The extent to which it will be appropriate to explain the day care arrangement to your child will depend upon her age. Below sixteen to eighteen months old (or even a bit older), it's not going to do any good to try to explain things much ahead of time. Below that age, repeated short explanations just prior to separation will be most appropriate. You may want to begin these explanations a day or two ahead of time, giving more detail and emphasis as the first day's separation is only a couple of hours away. Under about six months old, a clear "bye-bye" at the moment when you leave is about all you can plan.

The important thing is to gear the length and exhaustiveness of your explanation to the level of your child's understanding. Your child will, to some extent, derive comfort and security from the tone of your voice, especially just before departure. The important thing is for your demeanor to convey that everything's fine now, and will be fine after you leave.

Some caregivers recommend long explanations even to babies because of the comforting tone of voice, but I feel that really isn't necessary. Repeat your explanation as many times as you think your child needs in order to comprehend it. If your child is at the one- or two-word stage, teach him a few words to describe day care; for example, *day care* and the caregiver's name. If your child is talking, ask questions about what will happen. Then have your child repeat, to show she understands. For example, a mother and her twenty-month-old:

> MOTHER: Tomorrow, you're going to go to day care and play with kids again. To the house we went to the other day. It will be fun. . . . Tell me, what will you do tomorrow?
> CHILD: Fun with kids. Play? Sand?
> MOTHER: Yes, you can play in the sand again tomorrow, with the kids at day care. Can you say *day care?*
> CHILD: What? Day care?
> MOTHER: Mommy will go to work and Jessica will play with kids at day care while Mommy goes bye-bye.

And so on.

The idea here is to pair the coming separation with the idea that the child will be doing something nice while you are gone. For slightly older children, you may want to include a narrative of the whole day's routine, followed by a question and answer period. Toddlers enjoy knowing what will come next. It can be especially important for a two-and-a-half-year-old to know that he can watch *Sesame Street*, ask for a glass of milk, eat from his lunch box, go potty, and take a nap with his beloved blanket while in this new place.

The closer the first day's separation gets, the more you should focus on the explicit details of coming and going: "I will come in and play with you for a while, then I'm just going to watch you play and do whatever you want. Then, after a while, I'll need to go bye-bye. And then, you can keep right on playing, and soon, I'll be back again. I'll miss you when I go. . . ."

If your child lets you know that he will cry or be sad, or be upset, or that he doesn't want you to leave, you will need to explore those feelings with him. They are very natural feelings. The fact that your child can and will express them attests to his sensitivity and maturity. You can make suggestions to your child about how to handle negative feelings; for example, "You don't have to cry, because Daddy is going to come back," or "If you feel sad, you can ask the teacher to hold you for a while." Also, let your child know that you will miss him. You don't want him to feel that your love stops when you walk out the door.

The more you can tell your child about what to expect, provided he understands you, the better the resources he will have to remain emotionally at ease and unafraid of his new experience. This is important, because a child who is caught up in bad feelings is less likely to be receptive to the things he can be learning in his new environment. It's a kind of vicious circle. The more a child feels upset, the less likely he is to play, and the less likely he is to stop feeling bad.

There is a fine line between sources of fear and sources of curiosity in children. If you can reduce any anxiety your child may have, you allow natural curiosity and exploratory tendencies to take the upper hand, and he'll have a good time learning about his new day care arrangement.

PLANNING THE FIRST DAYS OF DAY CARE WITH YOUR CAREGIVER

What can your caregiver(s) do to help the separation process during the first few days of day care? You should discuss the caregiver's role with her prior to the first day. Some caregivers have strategies for helping children adjust. Others play it by ear. Often caregivers have adjustment strategies that really work well for them. Listen carefully to what they plan to do, and then decide whether that procedure is likely to suit you and your child. For example, some caregivers want mothers to leave right away, while others encourage them to stay a long time. Other caregivers make it their policy to let parents decide how to orchestrate the adjustment period.

In a day care center, you will want to find out which person will greet your child when he first arrives, and who he will be with when you leave. The important thing is that you and the caregivers know each other's plans, that you don't stand around at the last minute discussing details in front of your child. These details should have been ironed out during a preliminary visit, or a day or two ahead of time over the phone. Children are very sensitive to indecision and ambivalence. If a child senses that her parent is uncertain about how to behave in these unfamiliar circumstances, she may feel some degree of anxiety. It's not only important to consider *what* you say and do, but *how well* you carry it off. Having things straight with the caregiver beforehand makes the departure smoother and will convey to your child that you are in control of what's happening and that everything is fine.

THE STAGES OF A SEPARATION: DEPARTURE, ABSENCE, REUNION

Day care, as a psychological event, can be divided into three phases. The first phase is departure. This includes the words that are spoken before leaving, the act of going out the door, and the immediate reactions parents and children have to these events. The second phase is the actual absence, when parents and child are apart. The third phase is reunion. Reunion consists of the child becoming aware that the parents' return is imminent, the actual reunion, and the things that parent and child do in their first few moments back together.

How Long to Stay

In my research on adjustment to day care, I have been singularly impressed by the huge variation that both parents and teachers report for amounts of time that parents stay during the initial adjustment period ranging from those who choose or are required by caregivers to hand over the child and depart without even coming in, to those who stay all day for the first three days. At each extreme, and at all places in the middle, I have seen children adjusting well to day care.

What does this mean? That it doesn't matter what you do? No. It means that each child has his own requirements, and that some children are more sensitive than others to separation.

As a lower limit, you should stay at least an hour; a bit more for separation-anxious nine-to-fourteen-month-olds. One day of being there the whole time (for a short, half day), followed by a brief stay of one hour or so the following day, should be the upper limit of your stay in day care with your child. There really does seem to be a limit to "parental helpfulness," a point of saturation, at which the parent's continued presence in day care with the child starts to hinder, rather than help, the child's adjustment.

What do you do with your child while you are at day care with him? Exactly how do you help him adjust? Here are some hints:

- Do introduce him to other children.
- Do try and get him involved in toys.
- Do encourage him to explore on his own.
- Do stay low to the floor and available.
- Do stay tuned in to his activities.
- Don't hold or physically restrict him too much.
- Don't try to develop an activity for him that heavily involves you.
- Don't force or structure an interaction between your child and another (let them come to it themselves).
- Don't stand around and chat with the caregiver a great deal.
- Don't act like a teacher, playing with other children.

The idea is to be available but to be rather inconspicuous. Your child should be more aware of you than anyone else is. Your purpose for being there is to provide your child with a secure base from which to explore. You don't want your presence to stilt the activity of caregivers and other children. Don't really involve yourself in activities. If your child feels he must compete with other children for your attention, the new day care arrangement will seem all the more threatening.

Security Blankets   A child needs a transitional object. Transitional object? It is what cartoonist Charles Schultz has termed a security blanket. It is something of your child's that he can carry around as a representation of you and all that is familiar and homey. Children often develop intense feelings toward transitional objects. But some never do. If your child does, bring along the blanket, doll, or whatever for the first few days. Some centers and even family day care homes prefer that children not bring their own things so that there won't be problems with sharing. Nonetheless, a security blanket, even stuffed in a cubby or a diaper bag, can be a source of comfort if your child knows it's there, and can go look at it and touch it from time to time.

If your child doesn't have a transitional object, you may want to bring something familiar from home anyway. For a very little baby you might want to bring a mobile or something the baby looks at often. It will provide a sense of continuity. It may help the caregiver to calm the child if he becomes distressed. A couple of parents I have known have left the child's car seat at the day care mother's so that the child can travel in the day care mother's car. What these parents don't realize (consciously, at least) is that the car seat is an especially nice transitional object because it tells the child that he is going to be going in your car again, and reminds him that he'll be going home.

When You Leave

When parents think about leaving their child, their central goal is to minimize the stressfulness of the moment. Only a few studies have contributed to an understanding of how to reduce the stressful effects of separation. Most mother-child separation studies have focused on what the child does after the departure, rather than on what the child actually did during the time the mother was leaving.

Of course, you don't need a psychologist to tell you that some kids cry at departures and some don't. Or, that the ones who cry are more overtly disturbed by the separation than the ones who do not. But it is possible to look at departure behavior in a more subtle way. First you should understand that overt behavior is just one indicator of how a child is reacting. For example, one study reported that children who had their heart rates monitored during separations from their mothers showed increased physiological stress, even when they seemed outwardly calm. This is important for you to know in order to understand that even if your child seems unfazed by your departure, inwardly his body may be still registering stress — stress that ideally should be alleviated or minimized.

What's a mother to do? A reseach team at the Educational Testing Service in Princeton, New Jersey, suggested that the way a mother and child relate to one another just prior to departure may influence the amount of crying and distress when the mother does leave. They noticed that children who played independently prior to the mother's leaving were less distressed when she left than children who had been in physical contact with their mothers. This study suggests that a child should be playing on her own prior to the time parents leave. However, it may be that children who are able to play so easily when in an unfamiliar place just find separations inherently less stressful.

These researchers also found that mothers who tried to ease departure stress by giving the child something concrete to do before leaving had children who separated more easily. For example, one mother told the child to "play with the Tinker Toys — build me a house."

Saying Good-bye   The way parents play and talk to children prior to leaving can influence the intensity of departure protest. The most important recommendation concerning leave-taking is never to just slip out the door. *Always* say good-bye, no matter how old your child is. A child who observes that her parents sometimes leave when she simply turns her back, may get very anxious every time you walk out of the room for a minute. Parents who leave without saying good-bye spare their own pain. They are less likely to see and hear the child's departure protest. Just because the parent doesn't see it doesn't mean that it doesn't happen, or that it is any less painful for the child. Leaving without saying good-bye destroys a child's growing sense of trust, which is so important to secure development.

One thing parents can do to make departures easier is to give the child a task. In light of the fact that stress can manifest itself in reduced amount of play, this seems to be a particularly good idea. Alleviating the "symptom" (reduced playing) may not be the "cure," but it can help a young child to feel that the new environment provides opportunities for normalcy (i.e., continued play).

The task might be a ritual for handling the departure itself. For example, each day when Amanda, a three-year-old, was left in family day care, she carried out a ritual of a kiss, a hug, and blowing five kisses. Prior to the establishment of this routine, she was less sure exactly when her mother was leaving and how long the leave-taking would extend. Her tension would just build up. After a few months of carefully following this routine, Amanda began to be less rigid about it until her good-byes looked more typical. She no longer needed this behavioral security blanket. If you find it necessary, you might want to devise a similar transitional strategy that would appeal to your child.

For a younger child, you might want to pair your departure with something he finds comforting. Each day before Helene left six-month-old David to go to work, she would lay him in his crib and bring his morning bottle. He would be so engrossed in the bottle that he would observe her departure only briefly.

Other departure-time distractors include *Sesame Street*, breakfast, peers, and toys. An important element of successful departures is a high level of day-to-day repetition. When events are predictable, children tend to be less stressed.

Some children can benefit from initial one-to-two-hour separations, as warm-ups, before leaving "for real." You can think of this as priming your child to understand separation. Brief separations can provide children with concrete means of internally representing the departure, absence, reunion sequence. First you'll have to decide whether warm-up separations will be useful to your particular child. Some kids will be made more anxious by this than by a real separation. Mainly, this strategy may be most useful with five-to-ten-month-olds (or so), who can see that you are leaving, but don't comprehend verbal explanations about returning.

By the time a child is one and a half to two years old, you can give him a point of reference for your return by tying it to a familiar event in the day. For example: "Daddy will come to pick you up after your nap." You should realize that children do not have the same sense of the passage of time as we do, and that passing events are more real to them than the hour and minute hands on a clock.

The length of time spent saying good-bye may affect the amount of stress the child feels. One study has suggested that shorter good-byes may be better than longer ones. Although the study was made in a laboratory and lacked a demonstrable relation to real events, the conclusion seems to be warranted. Long explanations tend to include some information the child doesn't understand. A long message may seem more ambiguous than a short one. A child may be more likely to feel anxious about such long explanations, since they give fears about unfamiliar people and places time to build. A shorter good-bye nips these apprehensions in the bud.

Often the child starts to cry as you leave, so you stay and comfort him until he stops. Then, as you start to leave again, he starts to cry again. Each time this happens, it will probably get more and more difficult to calm your child. You just have to make the decision to leave, and do it. This may seem harsh, but it is the only way to teach your child what to expect. The more upset the child gets before you leave, the more difficult it will be for the caregiver to get him to calm down after you are gone. Make the actual leave-taking brief.

When You're Gone

It's important for you to know how your child acts during initial adjustment to day care. You will need to monitor his behavior by considering how he behaved when you left, when you returned, and what he was reported to have done while you were away.

You'll need to depend upon the caregiver's report. How reliable is a caregiver's report? Perhaps more reliable than you can sometimes easily believe. There is an amazing phenomenon that virtually all caregivers report and that I have repeatedly observed: many children cry when their parents leave them. Then ... they stop within thirty seconds of the mother's walking out the door! Most children do this! The crying is a message, a demonstration to the parent. The parent leaves to the sound of the child's crying, feeling awful, but it stops sooner than most ever imagine. It may help you to stand outside the door of the house, apartment, or classroom and listen for a few minutes. If you witness this amazing phenomenon of the turning off of the tears, you are bound to have any guilt allayed. What makes this whole thing worse is that many children get so excited when they hear their parent coming to get them at the end of the day, they burst out crying. Hence, the unfortunate parents of these children leave them crying and return to crying. Then the caregiver says, "She stopped crying the minute you left, and didn't cry again until a minute ago." "Fat chance," you think. But believe me, the caregiver is telling you the truth.

How long will the adjustment process take? A report of one- and two-year-olds attending day care centers for the first time addressed this issue. Children were observed on the first, fifth, and tenth days of care. On the first day, there were frequent stranger reactions and delays in beginning to play, more so in less securely attached children. By the fifth day these reactions had lessened; by the tenth day, these children were virtually indistinguishable from other children in their centers. They typically greeted the teacher, played, and did not cry.

Another study examined longer-term adjustment and found that parental avoidance and social-emotional adjustment problems diminished the longer a one- or two-year-old was in care. Some of my research showed that the frequency of interactions between one- and two-year-olds and their family day care mothers reached equilibrium between three and five months into the arrangement.

It is not atypical, and certainly not abnormal, for adjustments to take longer than a couple of weeks. What you should see are daily signs that your child's adjustment is growing and that he is developing ways of coping with the stress of separation. Find out whether he is playing, and whether the play sounds typical for him. You might expect that during the adjustment phase, play would "regress" a bit, that is, become less mature, less intense, and less complex. It just means that less than full attention is being paid to activity because the child is internally dealing with the idea of separation.

Once in a very great while, a child may not adjust to day care and appears to develop a severe emotional disturbance as a result of entering care. I have seen only one such child out of hundreds whom I've known to have shown a normal range of adjustment reactions. This girl, Danielle, was left full time beginning at age two and a half in a family day care home with one caregiver and ten or eleven other children under six years old. Danielle had seemed rather typical for her age when I visited her and her mother in her home, prior to starting day care. Less typical was the fact that she was still breast-feeding. Her first day of day care was also the day her mother began to wean her — cold turkey. Obviously, there were many complexities to this mother-child relationship, but day care started a real break in this child's normal development. She cried and sat in one place all day for the first month. After four months she would stay near other children but would play neither with them nor with toys. It's possible that severe problems would have arisen with this child had she never gone into day care. Day care may have been the catalyst that aggravated a potentially bad situation.

The chances of your child's having adjustment reactions as severe as Danielle's are extremely slim. If something like this does happen to you, you should consider changing day care arrangements, using a more individualized form of care, if possible. Or you should consider talking about your child's adjustment problem with a mental-health professional whose ideas about day care don't start and stop with the notion that a woman's place is only in the home. There's nothing wrong with asking for a little professional help to get you over rough spots.

When You Come Back

The reunion is psychologically important as a means of reestablishing contact with your child. It is an opportunity to catch up on your child's activities, as well as to focus on potential adjustment difficulties. One thing that is likely to affect your reunion is how long you were away, and how *you* felt during that time.

As a means of helping you understand just how deeply separations and reunions can affect mothers and children, I will tell you a primate story: sometimes, it's difficult for researchers to study what they want to study in humans, so they use monkeys as an analog. Mother-infant attachment in squirrel monkeys in many ways resembles that of humans. One group of researchers observed the separations and reunions of mother and infant squirrel monkeys who lived in a "family" cage with other monkeys. They biochemically analyzed stress in mothers and infants prior to, during, and after separations. They found that: 1) mothers and infants showed stress during separation whether or not they remained with their families or were put in isolation cages; 2) infants who stayed with the family during separation were often "aunted" (cared for) by another female; 3) aunted infants appeared outwardly calm, *but* biochemically looked as stressed as if they were all alone; 4) upon reunion, the mother's biochemistry quickly returned to normal while the infant's took much longer to do so.

What does this suggest? First, that separations are actually physically stressful to both mothers and children. (Maybe mothers keep pictures of their children on their desks at work to stay biochemically in balance.) Second, even though a child may behave as if he is perfectly well-adjusted in day care, he may, physiologically, still be experiencing stress. Third, when reunited, the mother should realize that her feelings of relief may not be matched in the child; that the child needs more time, more intense interaction, to feel equally relieved. This, of course, is all hypothetical for humans, although it makes good theoretical and intuitive sense.

You can make the initial separations shorter until your child develops a means for handling at least the overt, behavioral manifestations of stress. When you greet your child upon return, pay him exclusive attention for a while, as long as he seems to crave it. You can always greet the caregiver, or attend to gathering his things together, after you've been there a few minutes. When you return, pick your child up, hug him, establish a secure feeling of physical contact. Talk to him, reassure him that you are there to stay. The primate research suggests that this may help. It certainly can't hurt!

Think for a minute. What do you expect your child to do when you return after his first day in day care? Do you think he will be excited? Nonchalant? Ignore you? Will he want to leave right away, or stay and play longer? One way of estimating how well the first days have gone will be to see how your child's reunion behavior matches your expectation of it.

It is to be expected that during the initial few weeks of adjustment, more secure children may have less than secure-looking reunions. For example, you may expect clinginess or avoidance; babyishness or excessive independence. Just like normal adjustment to departure (e.g., decline in amount of crying), insecure reunion behavior should decrease over time. Give your child the time he needs to act out feelings of unsureness about the situation. Go along with what he wants you to do during that initial period of reunion. Allow your child to feel in control of the situation.

Many parents say that when they go to get their child or come home to their child they have the distinct feeling that the child is mad at them. Other parents note that their children are ambivalent: alternately happy to see them, then angry. It's fairly common for young children to hit parents at reunion. Don't get angry. Do read it as an "I'm mad!" message. Give your child some love and care, and the mad feelings are likely to transform into glad feelings.

The end of the day in day care can be really problematic. Your child is tired. You are tired. You both want to be home. It's easy for either you or your child to feel overwhelmed. Plan to slow your pace as you arrive home (if you have in-home care) or at the day care arrangement. Don't rush. The world won't collapse if you leave the day care arrangement ten minutes later and hit five minutes more traffic, or have to wait an extra twenty minutes for the next train.

You, as an adult, can make conscious efforts to relax. Children do not yet have the same degree of control over their feelings. Children need transitions to occur more slowly so they can comprehend and react appropriately to what's happening.

When children behave in some extreme way upon reunion, they are really using that behavior as a means of releasing a spring of tension that has been winding up all day during the separation. Some children, for example, become hyperactive when their mothers arrive, running around, showing her things, or increasing the pace of their play. Other children withdraw or become obstinate about leaving day care. These children are having trouble letting themselves relax and unwind.

Let your child take the lead in his method of releasing tension. If your child wants to show you around, or show what he's been doing, follow along. Be patient, and listen to all the things he wants to tell you about his day. If your child seems withdrawn or rejecting, approach him carefully, join in his activity slowly, giving him time to reaccept you on his terms. For a verbal child, you could ask questions about the day. Encourage your child to communicate and to describe what he's done. Your child may derive real security and satisfaction by just seeing you in the day care setting. It concretely demonstrates to him that you and day care are overlapping, linked, integral aspects of his life.

Your child's initial days of day care may be stressful for all parties involved. Just be prepared for it. Examine your own feelings about it. Talk about what you expect with your spouse and with the caregivers.

Children do cry. Expect it. Minimize your child's stress by anticipating his needs and meeting them in a way that is developmentally appropriate for his age. Explain as much as he will understand. Always say good-bye, don't just disappear. Always give a big hello when you come back again.

Adjustment can take time. Be prepared for it. Look for signs of increasing adjustment: decrease in departure protest, increase in play while you're gone, acknowledgment and joy at reunion. Talk to the caregiver about how things look to her. Reshape your strategy if your child needs more time (or less) to adjust than you anticipated.

Remember that your child will only reflect as much of a positive attitude about day care as you do. Loving your child can be demonstrated in ways that don't include being together twenty-four hours a day.

Day Care as the Status Quo

YOU'VE GOT YOUR DAY CARE arrangement off and running. You've made it through those few first tough days. Hurray! Now, all you have to do is maintain this wonderful status quo you've put so much effort into achieving. In order to do that, you should be aware of some of the difficulties that can crop up. First, how do you know when there's a problem with the day care arrangement, and what can you do about it? Second, how do you handle changes in family life that result from the smaller amount of time spent with your children?

*PARENT-CAREGIVER RELATIONS*_____

In some ways, a day care arrangement is like a new car. When you get it, you need to make a commitment to maintaining it, so that it will continue to perform well. Everyone is enthusiastic about keeping a car in shape when it's brand new. After it's broken in, it takes a certain amount of discipline to give it the same care. You'll need to establish a maintenance schedule to keep your day care arrangement "as good as new." Just as some car owners check their oil and battery each time they fill up their cars with gas, some parents spend time each day finding out how their child did. Other people check the oil less often, and are none the worse for it; some day care arrangements run well that way too. What is necessary is to judge, given your model of car, how often to check the oil, before it has a chance to get too low and your engine seizes. And with day care, it's up to you to decide how often to take time to speak with your caregiver(s) about your child, in order to avoid a buildup of problems or hard feelings.

Parents sometimes hesitate to speak directly and openly with caregivers. It does take a lot of energy. Instead, these parents say they rely on "vibes" they feel the caregiver puts out. Often, parents have told me that it's no use to discuss a particular problem with the caregiver, that they pretty much know how the caregiver would respond to any suggestion they might make. (Caregivers say the same thing about parents.) This isn't always true. Caregivers really appreciate frequent and frank communication with parents. If a caregiver begins to feel that a parent doesn't want to talk with her, it can affect her attitude toward that parent's child. Caregivers tend to be more cautious and guarded, less open and warm, when they think that the parents hold some unspoken grudge against them. You really don't want to get to the point where you are hesitant to talk to the caregiver and the caregiver is hesitant to talk to you because each is afraid of what the other thinks, or how the other may react.

If you are the type of parent who would like to talk to the caregiver on a structured, regular basis, you could include something right in your day care contract about when and how often you and your caregiver will get together. This will provide you with an assured channel for discussing your child and any incipient or current problems.

In the beginning, it will take a while for you to get a feel for what is happening to your child all day. Therefore, in the beginning, you may want a daily report: "How did he do?" "What did he play with?" "Whom did he play with?" "What did she have for lunch?" "How long did she nap?" These questions enable you to form a mental picture of what your child is doing during each part of the day, and will reassure you, as you move through your day. If you know what your child's been doing, you can adjust your expectations of your child when you are reunited. You'll know how tired he is, whether he needs to eat right away, how active he's been, whether he's been through any particularly tough times that day.

It's fairly easy to get updates on daily activities from a caregiver once you've established a pattern for doing it. What may be more difficult to extract are problems the caregiver may have in dealing with your child. This is especially true of home-based caregivers, who are often alone all day long without other adults. When you arrive, it's a big change of pace after hours of talking only to wee ones. It may take her a few moments to feel competent to communicate with an adult who's been out in the world of other adults all day. That's why it's good to have planned meeting times (say, once per week) to discuss how things are running.

If the caregiver knows you're going to be taking time to talk about your child, she will be able to prepare herself, make an agenda, and feel more at ease and appropriate about "complaints" she may want to register. Before a caregiver says critical things about a child, she usually tries to say some good things. So, it can take her a while to get to the topics that are most in need of discussion. Accept the good things as praises of your child-rearing skills and then ask about the bad things. For example: "Is William still taking Carla's snacks away from her?" "What have you been doing about it?" "Has that worked out well enough?" Or: "Has Meghan still been waking up after one hour of nap this week?" "Is she still bugging you about not going back down?" "It's OK with me for you just to tell her it's nap time and let her cry it out."

If directly questioned, the caregiver is more likely to be candid. You should also be aware that some caregivers are reluctant to influence some aspect of your child's behavior that they think you approve of (and they don't). For example, you may think that baby talk is cute. The caregiver may prefer to discourage it. When it's a subjective, qualitative gray area like that, with no clear right or wrong, some caregivers choose to bury the problem. But unresolved problems don't die, they just get sublimated. Caregivers do harbor resentments. (Parents do, too.) If they are not aired, they build up, and later seem disproportionately important to everyone.

In day care centers, the parent-caregiver communication process tends to work somewhat differently. There may be less opportunity for informal get-togethers. With many children around, plus the goings-on associated with drop-off and pick-up times, center caregivers have too many responsibilities to take much time out for parents. Being with the children is their most important job. A recent article noted that the track record for time spent by parents in the day care center was abysmally poor. The average parent spent 7.4 minutes per day in the center; 10 percent didn't even come in with their kids each morning! If you want a good time to talk informally with a caregiver, try going very early in the morning when most of the children aren't there yet; or better, in the afternoon after most have gone home.

Good centers hold periodic, individual parent conferences where one or more of the caregivers sits down with the parents and goes over what she feels are strong points, weak points, and future goals for the child. Typically, these parent conferences are held two to four times a year. These conferences are good for both parents and caregivers because they give parents an opportunity to understand how the caregivers approach their work, and they give the caregivers an opportunity to understand your child by knowing what you are like. A few formal parent-caregiver conferences should be supplemented by more regular weekly or biweekly informal visits.

In addition, there may be parents' nights for more informal discussions with caregivers and with other parents. Getting to know other parents who share your day care arrangement is yet another way of keeping in touch with what's happening there.

In day care centers, there is usually a great deal going on at pick-up and drop-off times. If you want to find out what's happening with your child, ask a caregiver who is often in the room with him. Don't rely on information from the director or head teacher if she is able to offer you only secondhand generalizations. Head teachers are in touch with major concerns in the class, but directors, if they aren't in the room with the children, are often not. (They may, however, be most anxious to do a public relations job on new parents.) If you feel that there are any problems that result from things the caregivers are doing (or not doing), go to the source. I assure you, going over the caregiver's head to her boss, right off the bat, will earn you no Brownie points with the staff. It won't help the quality of the care that your child receives either.

Talk directly with caregivers. If that doesn't have the desired effect, then talk to supervisors.

The most pragmatic reason for getting together with your child's caregiver is, of course, to discuss your child. As you and the caregiver get used to one another, you will develop a personal relationship. The quality, especially the openness, of such relationships is closely related to the success of the day care arrangement. That doesn't mean that your child's caregiver needs to become your intimate friend for your day care arrangement to succeed. (But I've certainly seen some lasting friendships develop between mothers and caregivers.) It does mean that you really shouldn't ignore the human qualities of the person or people that provide you with child care services. The caregiver's job is to provide loving care for your child. You owe her respect. Some parents approach caregivers with the same perfunctory attitude that others reserve for the machines that dry their clothes and wash their dishes.

In the most successful arrangements, parents and caregivers relate to each other as adults sharing a common interest. Other parents and caregivers, unfortunately, come to view each other more as rivals. The adults involved begin to feel that they are competing for the child's affection; or that they are competing for a prize that will go to the one who does the "best" job raising the child. The most unfortunate thing about rivalry between parents and caregivers is that it can color the children's perception of positive relatedness or contact between parents and caregivers. Children depend upon bilateral support by parents and caregivers. Children can become confused if they find themselves the object of adult rivalry. This situation occurs most often when the caregiver is a relative or friend of the family, someone emotionally involved with the child.

It's important for parents and caregivers to share a child-rearing values system. Children are sensitive to discontinuities in expectations that different sets of caregivers may have for them. Conflicting sets of demands might cause the child to feel confused, ambivalent, or resistant to adults.

More serious are conflicts children experience when parents try to block, negate, or minimize the affection they naturally develop for their caregivers: for example, if a child talks about his caregiver on the weekend, and the parent says, "Oh, let's not talk about *her* now!" That minimizes the caregiver's importance in the child's eyes. A different sort of example: "But Grandma, Daddy said I could have the candy bar I've been saving for after school today!" "When I'm here you'll do what *I* want, not what your Daddy said."

Competition between parents and caregivers is an extremely touchy subject. It affects parents in complex and subtle, and not-too-subtle, ways. The unconscious appeal of center day care, for many parents, is that there is much less chance that another single adult may seemingly replace the parents in the eyes of their child.

It's very natural and healthy for you to want your child to love you more than anyone else. But young children love to give love, as well as to be loved themselves. Part of the natural, adaptive process of developing from a helpless infant into a competent person has to do with the child's ability to engender in caregiving adults feelings of loving and a desire to provide care. Children can successfully have multiple attachments. As a parent, you need to accept that fact, and realize that just as a parent can love however many off-spring she or he has, a child can feel and act attached to a second-ary caregiver, without any diminution in the primary love for parents. A child's love is based on the exigencies of the moment: whom the child is with, what that person does for the child.

The kind of love a young child has for a caregiver is perhaps a forerunner of friendship. A parent's love for that child is somewhat different, based on knowledge that they have long-term responsibilities and ties, as well as the immediate role of caregiver. The way in which a young child expresses such early friendship may seem, to parents, to be the same as attachment to them. As children grow older, they learn the distinction between familial love and friendship.

Parents who acknowledge that a significant emotional tie may exist between their child and their child's caregiver seem to have less problem with jealous or competitive feelings toward the caregiver. The more parents come to know their child's caregiver and become friends, the less this is a problem. In other words, it's easier to "share" your child with someone you like than with someone you view as an antagonist or rival.

Mothers sometimes joke about the way their children relate to caregivers. This is a means of discharging some anxiousness about the development of these friendship/attachments: "Wanda loves being at Sue's so much that she doesn't want to come home with me in the afternoon." "I don't know why Jared cries when I come to get him; I think he must love Margaret better than he loves me." "Dave likes the teachers at day care so much he asks to go there on the weekends when I tell him he's staying home with us!" And the old favorite: "Marsha is perfectly potty-trained when Consuela is here, but doesn't ever want to do it for me."

A very high proportion of the time, children are not (as their parents may fear) confused about who their parents are. Rather, the seeming preference for the caregiver over the parent may reflect some confusion about who will take care of them when, and the differences between settings where Mommy and Daddy are, and where Mommy and Daddy are not.

Sometimes when a child expresses a desire to be in day care instead of at home, he may be doing this because time spent with parents is associated with the release of more intense and difficult-to-control feelings, which are more easily kept in check while the child is in day care. One of my studies showed that children and caregivers are more neutral and less emotionally expressive with each other than are children and parents. For some children, it may be difficult to let loose their emotions and to shift into high emotional gear when they come home.

THE CHILD'S REPORTS

If your child has begun to talk, you can use her to get information about adjustment to day care, what she likes and doesn't like. You can ask about what went on each day, giving little suggestive prompts: "Did you go outside?" "Did you play in the sand?" "Did you have stories?" Talking about your child's day is also a way of showing that you've been thinking about her. Talking about day care each day can also be a bridge between day care and home. The more you make a point of regularly asking about day care, the better your child will get at remembering and reporting.

There are some limitations to talking to children about day care. For one thing, they "lie." *Lie* may be too strong a word — perhaps *fantasize* or *prevaricate* is better. Children often have imaginations stronger than their memories. Perfectly plausible stories may be absolutely madeup. For example, Michelle, age two and a half years: "I had meatballs, orange juice, and noodles for lunch." Upon checking with the caregiver, her father discovered she had chicken, rice, and milk.

More of a problem are children who report stories of being abused by other kids, or ignored by teachers. While these stories could be true, you should do some checking with caregivers or other parents before taking a child's report at face value. Of course, young children don't tell these stories to be evil or deceptive; it's just "creative remembering." Children also have an undeveloped sense of the passage of time and may not report events in sequence or on the day they actually took place. Several events may blend in a child's memory and be reported as one occurrence.

One wise and very experienced Montessori nursery school teacher offers yet another explanation for the poor, spotty reports that children give of their daily activities: they love the sense of independence and control that comes from knowing something that the omniscient parent doesn't know. Young children glory in the feeling of power in keeping secrets.

You can sometimes interpret children's reports in a way similar to dream interpretation: there's a reason that the event was recalled or mentioned, but it is as likely to be oblique, symbolic, or reflective of a wish as it is to be real. For example, if your child continually reports (inaccurately) that other children hit him and take toys away from him, it may be that something related is bothering him. Maybe he observes other children playing together and is afraid to join in because he thinks he will be ignored or hurt. Try to look for the thread of truth in these fantasized reports.

WHEN THINGS LOOK BAD BUT REALLY AREN'T_____

Your day care arrangement is going along fine. But then suddenly, it seems as though your child's begun to hate it. Often, parents report they decided to change arrangements because all of a sudden the child began to scream when she was dropped off in the morning and seemed angry in the afternoon.

Interestingly, the parents who observe these changes in their child's behavior often happen to have children nine to twelve months old, or about one and a half to two years old. The nine-to-twelve-month-old period corresponds, of course, to the onset of stranger anxiety. The second peak, which is noted less often, may be a late arrival or second wave of the typical nine-to-twelve-month-old behavior. Psychoanalysts call this "rapprochement crisis" when it occurs in the middle of the second year. Just as the first phase of separation anxiety follows the onset of walking, the second phase seems to follow the onset of talking.

Typically, a deterioration in a child's seeming adjustment occurs in a child who has been in day care from a very early age; for example, since before six months old. Suddenly, the caregivers who were accepted as easily as parents, seem to become unacceptable. Rejection of the caregivers in favor of the parents is one sign that the primary attachment is to the parents. While it is reassuring to see such vital indicators of attachment, there is also a need to make your child feel better about being left.

The best thing that you can do is to follow the adjustment procedures just as if your child were starting day care for the first time: talk more about going to day care, about what's going to happen there, when you will return, and so on. You may want to spend some time with your child during day care hours, just to check on how the caregiver is handling this newly emerged personality. It can be frustrating when a previously easy child becomes more difficult. The caregiver will tend to feel less rewarded for the efforts she puts into the care of that child. Just reassure her that it's a temporary thing, and that with a little extra attention you expect that this too will pass.

WHEN TO CHANGE DAY CARE ARRANGEMENTS_____

Sometimes, despite your best efforts, an arrangement doesn't work out. Perhaps other children at the center don't mix well with your child. Maybe your housekeeper gets married and moves back to Portugal. Your day care mother's youngest starts first grade and she decides to finish college. A caregiver has responded so poorly to a crisis that she has entirely breached your trust in her. You decide that your child is not ready for a group setting. Whatever the reason, your plans change, or the caregiver's plans change, and that day care arrangement can no longer continue. Some day care arrangements run a natural course. The child outgrows it.

How do you decide to make a change? Rule number one: don't decide in haste. Remember that stability may be quite important to your child. Anytime you contemplate a change, try to calculate a benefits-to-risks ratio with your child in mind. Just how intolerable is what you have? Is the thing that's bothering you something the caregiver does to you, or something she does to the child? How easily does your child adjust to day care? Are you or your child prepared to go through the adjustment process again? Ask yourself these questions before you burn your bridges.

If the caregiver has said something that irritates you, try not to fly off the handle. Ask for an explanation or for constructive suggestions. What does she think would be better? If you have some sort of confrontation with your caregiver, allow at least an overnight cooling-off period.

If the differences are irreconcilable or non-negotiable, you'll need to look for a new arrangement.

I've seen mothers cut off their noses to spite their faces: they quit one arrangement before finding another. When this happens, the mother or father is likely to miss at least some work. Then, the selection of a new day care arrangement is harried, with great pressure to select the first seemingly adequate situation that comes along.

Even if it is apparent to you that you need to terminate your current arrangement, you owe the caregiver or center the courtesy of one to two weeks' notice. That will give you time to look. It will give the caregiver or center director time to refill your child's slot. What may not be right for you may be fine for someone else.

If you end an arrangement because your caregiver or center can no longer keep up their end of the agreement, they owe you the courtesy of one month to two weeks' notice. If you are going to be looking for a new arrangement because the caregiver can no longer provide care, you may want to consider looking for new care, jointly, with other families that share your current child care arrangement. There are a couple of advantages to doing this. First, you can divide up the work of locating choices, preliminary interviewing, and so on. Second, and more important, if you can keep the children together going into a new arrangement, they will have a greater sense of familiarity and security as they adjust to the new situation. It can be important to your child to have his friendships maintained at a time when other things are changing.

Recognizing Caregiver Burnout

Some day care arrangements end because the caregiver or day care center staff doesn't provide the quality of care that originally existed. A great deal has been written about worker burnout in a number of jobs. One researcher has identified three signs of job burnout among people who care for other people. These are: 1) emotional exhaustion, 2) feelings of depersonalization toward the children, and 3) loss of a sense of personal accomplishment.

It's not difficult to recognize the signs of burnout if you know what to look for. First of all, look for any changes in the regular routine of things. Has the caregiver begun to put the *Today* show on first thing each morning, instead of *Sesame Street*? Do you arrive in the afternoons to find her talking on the phone? Is she taking less care in her appearance? Does she complain that she doesn't have long enough or frequent enough vacations; or that the one she has just returned from seems as though it never was? A caregiver who tells you that she feels tired from early in the morning straight through the entire day, drinks coffee or smokes cigarettes incessantly, gets frequent headaches or other unexplained ills, may be showing signs of emotional exhaustion. A caregiver who ceases to see children as individuals, but rather as a demanding group whose needs are never satisfied, may be experiencing burnout in a slightly different way. Another caregiver's burnout may be experienced as children not relating to her personally — that she is merely the hand with the cookie in it, and not one person doing a nice thing for another person. A caregiver who lacks a sense of personal accomplishment from her work may feel that nothing she does really matters, that the day-to-day happiness of children is not really important. She may feel that the children do not notice her and do not appreciate her special efforts.

Pay attention to these qualitative ways in which the caregiver talks with you about herself, the children, and her job. Many factors contribute to burnout: low pay, low status, poor rewards for a job well done, lack of adult contact, and not enough variety in daily tasks and responsibilities. Personal and family problems can certainly color a caregiver's feelings about her job, too.

In a day care center, watch the job turnover rate. Often, when one or two caregivers leave, others follow. In a center, burnout is best taken up with the director. Ask if there is any way that you can help. Sometimes, it is precisely the lack of feedback from parents that makes caregivers feel that their work is less than meaningful. Some day care centers try to alleviate burnout by using a rotating staff structure. This means that each staff member divides time between playground, indoor play, the nursery, meal preparation, and so on. Caregivers change these job assignments on different days of the week or weeks of the month.

If you see signs of burnout developing in your child's caregiver, you may want to discuss them gently with her. Unfortunately, it often seems that the better caregivers are more susceptible to burnout than the more mediocre ones. If there is no way that you can help improve caregiver morale, it may be time to move on.

Changes in Developmental Needs of the Child

A few developmental milestones mark times at which a child's need for stimulation from the environment may change rather quickly. It would be a shame, though, to give up a really good caregiver or a superlative arrangement solely because of developmental change.

It may be possible to expand your child's horizons by planning trips; adding new activities, such as going to a play group; acquiring new toys and playing with old ones in new ways. If you have an in-home or small family day care arrangement, and want more opportunities for your child to be with peers, you might be able to work a couple mornings per week of preschool into your schedule. Maybe your caregiver or the preschool could provide mid-day transportation if you're not available. Adding new experiences a few at a time is usually better received by the child than sudden major changes.

If you do change care arrangements in order to provide a more challenging day care environment, you can try to take advantage of naturally occurring interruptions in care. Rather than changing care all of a sudden, you may want to wait until there is some sort of break or vacation when your child would have stopped going for a while anyway. For instance, if you are a teacher, and have the summer off, you might end one arrangement in June and begin another in September. Even a two-week vacation can serve as such a time divider. Every break in care of a week or more will require a certain amount of reacclimatization, anyway.

Changes in Parent-Child Relations

Will day care change the way you and your child feel toward one another? No one knows for sure. It's impossible to know what things would have been like for any one family had they not used day care.

One healthy thing that day care seems to accomplish is circumventing the tendency some mothers have to live their lives through their children. Many parents of day care children with whom I have talked seemed more likely to view even very young children as separate human beings, rather than as extensions of themselves. This, in fact, is true, because the child's experiences *are* separate, rather than only an extension of the parents' experiences.

In a positive sense, the perception of separateness can foster a child's feelings of individuality and independence. What I worry about is the child who may develop a negative sense of separateness (i.e., anxious attachment) because the parent is too cut off from him. Some parents may tend to resist the formation of a close bond with the child because day care and separation were imminent even before the birth of the child.

Most of the time, other qualitative changes in the parent-child relations take a less readily identifiable form than the more conspicuous development of an anxious attachment. Instead, there may be less serious "warning" signs that parents and children may be drifting apart. You can watch out for these indications that you may need to focus more on your child; for example, a mother observes her child drinking perfectly out of a cup for the first time, at the day care center. She reports that she had no idea her daughter knew how to do that. Sometimes, parents who aren't with their children much don't catch the cues that the child is ready to do a new thing, such as holding a cup. Also, a mother who doesn't mop up spilled milk twenty times a day may be less motivated to teach appropriate use of a cup than a mother who does.

Similarly, a mother who is with her child more often may repeatedly observe her child grasping blocks or rattles with handles, and get the idea to try out a cup. Another mother who just isn't there to observe much of her child's playtime might not get that idea and keep on offering bottles. Compounding this is the difficulty of working all day and then being patient enough to teach your child something entirely new when neither you nor your child are at your best.

There is a second, related point that needs to be made in regard to that same mother who comes to the day care center and observes her child using a cup for the first time. Time and time again, I've heard such mothers say, "What a great day care center; they've taught her to drink from a cup!" Credit can be given where it's due — the center should be teaching eight-month-olds to drink from cups. But all children learn to do that sooner or later, even with minimal supervision and teaching. Your child's development will almost inevitably progress, regardless of what care you choose. Try to distinguish what your child is being taught in his arrangement from what he is learning, naturally, on his own. If you are a first-time parent, it will be particularly difficult for you to know the difference between learning that is fostered by good-quality care, and inevitable acquisition of independence.

Parents of children in day care frequently report that developmental milestones occurred before they knew it. Comparatively, parents who stay at home seem more likely to report that each developmental milestone "took forever." For example: "Before I knew it he was cruising and then walking," versus "For a long time there, I thought she'd never learn to walk." This difference in how you perceive your child's rate of development seems to be related to the quantity of time that day care users compared to non–day care users spend with their children.

The diminished number of hours spent with day care children is not a problem, per se. Most child psychologists would agree that the quality of a parent and child's time together is probably more important than quantity. Many parents who use day care reason that they can compensate for lost time by creating opportunities for high-quality interactions in the evenings and on weekends. This is an admirable and important goal but the reality is that most parents may not be able to do this consistently, despite their best intentions.

Working parents usually have household responsibilities as well as their work responsibilities. (A lucky minority of you have housekeepers who can clean and cook and minimize further time away from your child.) Because of the time most parents have to spend attending to household affairs, my impression has been that the early morning and early evening parenting experiences of day care children are not better than those of children who've been home with their mothers all day. The preliminary findings of a study in progress address issues related to the quality versus quantity of parental care of day care children and suggests, for example, that dinner-time parent-child interactions of day care and home-raised children are not much different.

Planning the Mornings and Evenings Perhaps the worst times of day for families who use day care are mornings before work, and evenings just after you arrive home. Mothers often report that these are the most trying times of day — times when they are torn between paying attention to their children and seeing that necessary household tasks are accomplished. Bad experiences for children at these times can set a tone that may be hard to change for hours to come. With a little advance planning, dividing up of responsibilities, and setting of routines, everyone in your household should be able to survive these times with a minimum of discomfort.

While many working families feel that mornings and evenings are the most difficult times of day, they also feel that these are the most important times for children to know that parents are available. Children seem to be the most emotionally vulnerable at times when they are sleepy and hungry. Meeting the child's needs during these critical, more vulnerable periods, in a loving fashion, seems to go a long way in cementing the parent-child bond.

If possible, make time to be with your child for a few minutes when he gets up. Let him wake up slowly, hold him, nurse him, rock him, lay down with him until he's really awake. Then let the mad rush begin. Any child who starts the day feeling loved and secure about what is going on is getting off on the right foot. If your time is really short in the morning, you may find it preferable to bring your child to day care in his pajamas and without breakfast (if he can eat it there), then to forgo a few quiet moments together when he wakes up.

Plan your morning around your child's wake-up time. Try to adjust your child's bedtime to make wake-up time neither too early nor too late. Keep the same bedtime each weeknight so that you can plan your morning accordingly. Of course, little children have never heard of schedules, so your best plans can quickly fall apart when a cranky child refuses to cooperate. In some families, the parents wake up, dress, prepare breakfast, get older children ready, before the little one wakes up. That way they can devote undivided attention to readying him. Older children can roll with the punches in the morning, but the hubbub of activity can bewilder a child under two or three. Parents can take turns. One is in charge of the child awhile. The other does the chores. Alternately, with a baby, you can give at least part of a bottle in the crib, so your baby remains stationary while you do your morning chores.

The most important thing is to establish a predictable routine that doesn't include unnecessary strain on everyone's nerves. Little kids simply can't appreciate why being at work by 9:00 can be so much more important than being there at 9:15 or 9:30. They can't really understand why they are being rushed. A twenty-month-old who is denied the (infinite) amount of time necessary to put on his own socks is apt to take your doing it for him rather poorly. You don't need to get up at 5:00 A.M. so your child can put on his own socks, but *do* leave enough time so that you can "help" him, or explain why you need to do it for him. (You can compensate by promising to set aside an hour in the evening so that he can put on his own pj's.)

Your child should know what comes next and what is expected of him. You need to plan your time well. Dispense with chores that can wait if doing them will make your child feel rushed and as though he's just in the way. For example, you can bathe children the night before, prepare lunches the night before, have clothes laid out and ready to go, and so on.

The evenings can be similarly difficult. The same rules as for mornings apply. There should be a routine of expected events. It is especially nice to save some very individual time for your child. Put aside any unnecessary tasks until after your child's bedtime. Evenings are a great time for children and parents to learn to relax with one another.

Early evenings before dinner are a time of day when many parents find they may have to compromise on the quality of care they can offer their children. If you come home with a hungry kid at 6:00 P.M., there is no way it will do any good to sit down on the floor and play games with him. You need to prepare dinner. He needs to eat.

You may prefer your whole family to eat together. This may have to be forfeited for younger children if you come home from work fairly late. You can try giving bits of dinner prior to the meal to stave off hunger and crankiness. Coping with your child at 6:30 can be so much easier if that child has a fully belly and not a hungry one!

The nationally known saviors of the dinner hour are, of course, *Sesame Street* and *Mister Rogers' Neighborhood.* These may be the answer for you, if your child is over fourteen to sixteen months old. These shows are expert at retaining a child's interest and teaching (or reinforcing) things they are learning in other contexts. The dinner hour showings of these programs are tailored to the needs of working parents. If you have a television near where you are cooking or cleaning, you can discuss these shows with your children, making them even more of an educational experience. If you are very clever, you may learn to get dinner on the table just as Big Bird says, "*Sesame Street* has been brought to you today by the letter. . . ."

After dinner, I think it's really important that children who are in day care all day have some intensive, one-to-one time with their parents. Reading, talking, and other quiet activities tend to be well received at this time of day. It is an ideal time to get in some loving. It's an important time for parents to establish themselves as the number-one people in the hearts and minds of their children.

Some parents ask whether such intensive time can make up for being away all day. This isn't the issue so much as what type of parent-child relationship results from raising a child that way. One way that parents can understand this is through an analogy. Think of what it would have been like for you when you were a child, to have had two father figures instead of one father and one mother. (This assumes that you came from, or had familiarity with, the typical father-as-breadwinner, mother-as-housewife family of decades past.) Children of these prototypical nuclear families knew their father as someone who appeared in the evenings and weekends and did fun things with them. If you came from such a family, you can think of the different ways you felt toward your mother and toward your father and try to imagine how you would have felt differently toward your parents had they both played that role of "father."

Afterword

PARENTS MOST OFTEN ASK, "Is day care going to harm my child?" That is, "Will it affect development now?" "Will there be lasting effects?" For most children it seems that there are few immediate negative influences of day care. Less often, parents ask, "Will day care help my child develop?" There is not much evidence that day care is responsible for many significant short- or long-term gains in most children.

Becoming a user of day care brings you face to face with what may best be described as a quality-of-life issue. Parents want their children to be happy and content here and now. When you give your full effort to finding the best possible day care for your child, you can be really sure of one thing: that your child's life for the present is as happy and full as you can make it. That is a substantial accomplishment in and of itself.

You now have the information you need to make a sensible choice of day care arrangements. If you integrate this information with your own intimate knowledge and understanding of your child, you're not likely to go wrong. Adding your own knowledge to the things you've learned here is important not only because of your autonomy as a parent, but also because research on day care and child development is incomplete. A child's parents are in the unique position of being able to add their understanding of their child's individual differences to what is known about the development of children in general.

It's important that you think of yourself as a capable, independent decision maker, and of your child as an individual with a unique set of needs. Make your own decisions about day care. Don't just follow along with what friends have done, or with what relatives recommend. Whatever day care arrangement you choose, both you and your spouse should feel comfortable with the choice and subsequently comfortable with the quality of care that your child receives.

Child Care Information and Referral Agencies by State

Alabama

(county office)
Department of Pensions and Security
(county seat)

Alaska

Division of Family and Youth Services
Department of Health and Social Services
Pouch H-05
Juneau, Alaska 99811
(907)465-3206
OR
Department of Community and Regional Affairs
Local Government Assistance Division
225 Cordova Street, Building B
Anchorage, Alaska 99501
(907)276-1721

Arizona

Department of Health Services
Bureau of Day Care Licensing
1740 West Adams
Phoenix, Arizona 85007
(602)225-1112

Arkansas

Arkansas Social Service Day Care Licensing Division
Central Office
P.O. Box 1437
Blue Cross/Blue Shield Building
Seventh and Gaines
Little Rock, Arkansas 72203
(501)371-7512

California

Community Care Licensing Division
Department of Social Services
1232 Q Street
Sacramento, California 95814
OR
Northern California Resource and Referral Network
320 Judah Street
San Francisco, California 94122
(415)661-1714

Colorado

Colorado Department of Social Services
1575 Sherman Street
Denver, Colorado 80203
(303)866-3362

Connecticut

Office of Child Day Care
1179 Main Street
Hartford, Connecticut 06101
(203) 566-2893

Delaware

United Way Information and Referral Service
Porter State Service Center
511 West 8th Street
Wilmington, Delaware 19801
(302) 575-1052

Florida

(county office)
United Way Center
(county seat)
OR
Telephone Counseling and Referral Service
P.O. Box 20169
Tallahassee, Florida 32304
(904) 224-6333

Georgia

State Department of Human Resources
Child Care Licensing Section
618 Ponce de Leon Avenue, N.E.
Atlanta, Georgia 30308
(404) 894-4142

Hawaii

Child Care Switchboard
1352 Liliha Street
Honolulu, Hawaii 96817
(808) 935-1077

Idaho

(local office)
Division of Social Services
Department of Health and Welfare

Illinois

Department of Children and Family Services
Office of Child Development
1 North Old Stage Capitol Plaza
Springfield, Illinois 62706
(217) 785-2459

Indiana

Marian County Department of Public Welfare
141 South Meridian
Indianapolis, Indiana 46225
(317) 633-3876

Iowa

Children's Bureau
Iowa Department of Social Services
Hoover State Office Building, Fifth Floor
Des Moines, Iowa 50319
(515) 281-5657

Kansas

Wichita Child Care Association
155 South Hydraulic
Wichita, Kansas 67211
(316) 265-0871

Kentucky

Department of Human Resources
Office of the Inspector General
Division of Licensing
142 Chenoweth Lane
Louisville, Kentucky 40207
(502) 893-3678

Louisiana

Licensing and Certification
333 Laurel Street, Sixth Floor
Baton Rouge, Louisiana 70821
(504) 342-5773

Maine

Bureau of Resource Development
Licensing Division
Department of Human Services
221 State Street
Augusta, Maine 04333
(207) 289-3456

Maryland

Maryland State Department of
Health and Mental Hygiene
Division of Child Day Care
201 West Preston
Baltimore, Maryland 21201
(301) 383-4009

Massachusetts

The Office for Children
120 Boylston Street
Boston, Massachusetts 02111
(617) 727-8900

Michigan

Office for Young Children
701 North Logan, Suite 435
Lansing, Michigan 48914
(517) 371-3430

Minnesota

Minnesota State Department of
Public Welfare
Centennial Building
St. Paul, Minnesota 55155
(612) 296-3971

Mississippi

Mississippi State Board of Health
P.O. Box 1700
Jackson, Mississippi 39205
(601) 982-6505

Missouri

Day Care Licensing Unit
Division of Family Services
P.O. Box 88
Jefferson City, Missouri 65103
(314) 571-2450

Montana

Social Rehabilitation Services
Licensing Division
1211 Grand Avenue
Billings, Montana 59102
(406) 252-5601

Nebraska

(county or multi-county office)
County Department of Public Welfare
(county seat)
OR
Nebraska State Department of
Public Welfare
301 Centennial Mall South, Fifth
Floor
Box 95026
Lincoln, Nebraska 68509
(402) 471-3121

Nevada

Nevada Child Care Service Bureau
505 East King Street, Room 603
Carson City, Nevada 89710
(702) 885-5911

New Hampshire

New Hampshire Division of Welfare
Bureau of Child and Family Services
Hazen Drive
Concord, New Hampshire 03301
(603) 271-4395

New Jersey

Bureau of Licensing
Division of Youth and Family Services
1 South Montgomery Street
Trenton, New Jersey 08625
(609) 292-1878

New York

New York State Department of Social Services
40 North Pearl Street
Albany, New York 12207
OR
New York City Agency for Child Development Information Service
240 Church Street, Room 113
New York, New York 10007
(212) 553-6423/24/25

North Carolina

Statewide Care-line
Tollfree (800) 662-7030

North Dakota

County Social Service Office
(county seat, except Billings and Slope counties)
OR
Social and Rehabilitation Services Center
Randal Building
Rural Route 1, Highway 83
Bismark, North Dakota 58505
(701) 224-2304

Ohio

Day Care Licensing Unit
Ohio Department of Welfare
30 East Broad Street, 30th Floor
Columbus, Ohio 43215
(614) 466-3822

Oklahoma

(county office)
Division of Human Services
(county seat)

Oregon

Children's Services Division
198 Commercial Street, S.E.
Salem, Oregon 97310
(503) 378-3178

Pennsylvania

Day Care Division
State Office Building, Room 502
1400 Spring Garden Street
Philadelphia, Pennsylvania
Philadelphia: (215) 351-5603
other counties: (215) 238-7540

Rhode Island

Department of Children and Their Families
Day Care Licensing
610 Mount Pleasant Avenue
Providence, Rhode Island 02908
(401) 227-2804

South Carolina

(county office)
South Carolina Department of Social Services
(county seat)

South Dakota

Office of Children, Youth and Family Services
Department of Social Services
Kneip Building
Illinois Street
Pierre, South Dakota 57501
(605) 773-3227

Tennessee

Tennessee Department of Human
  Services
111 Seventh Avenue North
Nashville, Tennessee 37203
(615) 741-3284

Texas

Neighborhood Centers–Day Care
  Association
5005 Fannin
Houston, Texas 77004
(713) 529-3931

Utah

Department of Social Services
Field Services Division of Family
  Services, Children, Youth and
  Families
150 West North Temple, Room 370
Salt Lake City, Utah 84103
(801) 533-7123

Vermont

Vermont Department of Social and
  Rehabilitative Services
Licensing and Regulation Unit
103 South Main Street
Waterbury, Vermont 05676
(802) 241-2158

Virginia

Licensing Division
Department of Welfare
Commonwealth of Virginia
Blair Building
88007 Discovery Drive
Richmond, Virginia 23288
(804) 281-9204

Washington

Department of Social and Health
  Services
Bureau of Children's Services
State Licensor-0B41-D
Olympia, Washington 98504

Washington, D.C.

Rosemount Center
2000 Rosemount Avenue, N.W.
Washington, D.C. 20010
(202) 265-9889

West Virginia

West Virginia Department of Welfare
1900 Washington Street, East
Charleston, West Virginia 25305
(304) 348-7980

Wisconsin

(regional office)
Division of Community Services
Wisconsin Department of Health
  and Social Services

Wyoming

Wyoming Information and Refer-
  ral Service
1780 Westland Road
Cheyenne, Wyoming 82001
Cheyenne: (307) 635-4105
Tollfree: (800) 442-2744

Appendix B

Chapter References

It is not possible to list all the sources that have been valuable in the preparation of this book. This section lists specific studies and their findings by chapter and page, in the order cited.

INTRODUCTION

p. 5 *Number of children under six with working mothers:* Waldman, E., Grossman, A. S., Hayghe, H., and Johnson, B. L. "Working mothers in the 1970's." *Monthly Labor Review,* Oct. 1979, 39–49.

p. 5 *1985 projections for day care use:* Hill, C. R. "Private demand for child care: Implications for public policy." *Evaluation Quarterly* 2, 1978, 523–545.

p. 6 *1990 projections for mothers in the labor force:* Zigler, E. F., and Gordon, E. W. "Preface." In *Day Care: Scientific and Social Policy Issues.* Boston: Auburn House, 1982, v–ix.

p. 6 *1990 projections for day-care use:* Hofferth, S. L. "Day care in the next decade." *Journal of Marriage and the Family,* August 1979, 644–658.

CHAPTER ONE: WHAT TYPES OF CHILD CARE ARRANGEMENTS ARE AVAILABLE?

p. 8 *A family day care mother's view of family day care:* Sale, J., and Torres, Y. *"I'm not just a babysitter."* Unpublished paper, Pacific Oaks College, Pasadena, CA, 1971.

p. 11 *"Motherese":* Newport, E. "Motherese: The speech of mothers to young children." In N. J. Castellan, D. B. Pisoni, and G. Potts, eds., *Cognitive Theory,* vol II. Hillsdale, NJ: Lawrence Erlbaum Associates, 1977.

p. 13   *Pasadena study of family day care:* Sale, J. *"Open the door . . . See the people: A descriptive report of the second year of the Community Family Day Care Project."* Report for Children's Bureau, Office of Child Development, USDHEW, 1972.

p. 13   *St. Paul study of family day care:* Wattenberg, E. "Characteristics of family day care providers: Implications for training." *Child Welfare* LVI, no. 4, 1977, 211–229.

p. 13   *Maternal deprivation studies:* Provence, S., and Lipton, R. *Infants in Institutions.* New York: International Universities Press, 1962.
and
Freud, A., and Burlingham, D. *Infants without Families.* New York: International Universities Press, 1944.

p. 14   *National Day Care Study:* Abt Associates. *Final Report of the National Day Care Study: Children at the Center,* Vol. I. Cambridge, MA: Abt Associates, 1979.

p. 18   *Latchkey kids:* Ruderman, F. *Child Care and Working Mothers.* New York: Child Welfare League, 1968.

p. 19   *Child caregivers in the Third World:* Whiting, B. B., and Whiting, J. W. M. *Children of Six Cultures.* Cambridge, MA: Harvard University Press, 1975.

p. 26   *Influences on mothering style:* Hess, R. D., and Shipman, V. C. "Early experience and the socialization of cognitive modes in children." *Child Development* 34, 1965, 869–86.

p. 26–27   *Day care stability:* Emlen, A. C., Donoghue, B. A., and Clarkson, Q. D. "The stability of the family day care arrangement: A longitudinal study." Report to Research and Evaluation Division, Children's Bureau, USDHEW, 1971.
and)
Emlen, A. C., and Watson, E. L. "Matchmaking in family day care: A descriptive study of the day care neighbor service." Report to Research and Evaluation Division, Children's Bureau, USDHEW, 1971.

p. 32   *Schemes:* Piaget, J. *The Origins of Intelligence in Children.* New York: International Universities Press, 1952.

p. 33   *Amount of time spent with children by mothers versus family day care mothers:* Siegel-Gorelick, B., Ambron, S., and Everson, M. "Qualitative versus quantitative differences in caregivers in family day care and at home." Biennial International Conference on Infant Studies, New Haven, CT, 1980.

p. 35   *Age mixing versus age segregation in day care centers:* Fein, G., and Clarke-Stewart, A. *Day Care in Context.* New York: Wiley, 1973.

p. 36   *National Day Care Home Study:* Stallings, J., Wilcox, M., and Gillis, G. "National Day Care Home Study: Phase II Pilot Study." Report for Administration for Children, Youth and Families, USDHEW, 1978.
and
Divine-Hawkins, P. "Family Day Care in the United States: National Day Care Home Study Final Report." USDHHS, DHHS Pub. no. (OHDS) 80-30287, 1981.

p. 37–38 *Federal Interagency Day Care Requirements* (FIDCR) (*older, enacted standards*): Federal Panel on Early Education. "Federal Interagency Day Care Requirements." Washington, D.C.: Office of Economic Opportunity, USDHEW, 1968.
and
(*revised, unenacted standards*)
"USDHEW Day Care Regulations." Federal Register, Vol. 45, No. 55, Wed., March 19, 1980.

p. 38 *Critique of run-for-profit day care centers:* Featherstone, Joseph. "Kentucky Fried Children." *New Republic*, Sept. 5, 1970.

p. 39 *"Open" versus "closed" day-care programs:* Prescott, E. "A Comparison of Three types of Day Care and Nursery School-Home Care." Biennial meeting of the Society for Research in Child Development, Philadelphia, PA, 1973.

p. 39–40 *Swedish study comparing different types of day care:* Cochran, M. "A comparison of group day and family child-rearing patterns in Sweden." *Child Development* 48, 1977, 707–720.

p. 39–40 *Massachusetts study of center day care and home care:* Rubenstein, J. L., and Howes, C. "Caregiving and infant behavior in day care and in homes." *Developmental Psychology* 15, 1979, 1–24.

p. 41 *Review of day care research up to 1978:* Belsky, J., and Steinberg, L. "The effects of day care: A critical review." *Child Development* 49, 1978, 929–949.

p. 41 *Review of day care research after 1978:* Belsky, J., Steinberg, L. D., and Walker, A. "The Ecology of Day Care." In M. Lamb, ed., *Child-rearing in Non-Traditional Families.* Hillsdale, NJ: Lawrence Erlbaum, 1981.

p. 41 *Negative effects of infant day care in preschoolers:* Schwarz, J. C., Strickland, R. G., and Krolick, G. "Infant day care: Behavioral effects at preschool age." *Developmental Psychology* 10, 1974, 502–506.

p. 41 *Peer play in children attending day care centers:* Rubenstein, J., and Howes, C. "The effects of peers on toddler interaction with mothers and toys." *Child Development* 47, 1976, 597–605.

p. 41 *Peer aggression in day care centers:* Ambron, S., Siegel-Gorelick, B., and Everson, M. "An observational study of center day care, family day care, and home-rearing for toddlers." Unpublishd manuscript, 1982.

*CHAPTER TWO: PRACTICAL CONSIDERATIONS THAT MAY INFLUENCE YOUR CHOICE OF CHILD CARE*_____

p. 44 *Industry-based day care models:* Verzaro-Lawrence, M., LeBlanc, D., and Hennon, C. "Industry-Related Day Care: Trends and Options." *Young Children* 37, 2, 1982, 4–12.

p. 56–58 *Source of cost data for different types of day care:* Siegel-Gorelick, B. "State Survey of Day Care Practices." Questionnaire, Stanford University, 1981.

CHAPTER THREE: DETERMINING YOUR INDIVIDUAL CHILD'S DAY CARE NEEDS_____

p. 75   *Piaget's concept of object permanence:* Piaget, J. *The Construction of Reality in the Child.* New York: Basic Books, 1954.

p. 76   *Person permanence and attachment:* Bell, S. M. "The development of the concept of the object as related to infant mother attachment." *Child Development* 41, 1970, 291-311.

p. 78   *Motherese as a promoter of language learning:* de Villiers, P. A., and de Villiers, J. G. *Early Language.* Cambridge, MA: Harvard University Press, 1979.

p. 78   *Young children simplifying speech for even younger children:* Shantz, M., and Gelman, R. "The development of communication skills: Modification in the speech of young children as a function of the listener." *Monographs of the Society for Research in Child Development* 152, 1973.

p. 78   *Difficulty in language learning:* Bard, B., and Sachs, J. "Language acquisition patterns in two normal children of deaf parents." Boston University Conference on Language Acquisition, 1977.

p. 80-81   *Multiple attachments:* Schaeffer, H. R., and Emerson, P. E. "The development of social attachments in infancy." *Monographs of the Society for Research in Child Development* 29(a), 1964.

p. 81   *Synopsis of early work on maternal deprivation:* Bowlby, J. "Maternal Care and Mental Health." Geneva, World Health Organization, 1951.

p. 81   *Effects of several weeks' separations:* Heincke, C. M., and Westheimer, I. J. *Brief Separations.* New York: International Universities Press, 1965.

p. 81   *The following are seven studies that all examined day care and some aspects of mother-child attachment, and have aided in identifying potential risk factors:*

• Doyle, A., and Somers, K. "The effects of group and family day care on infant attachment behaviors." *Canadian Journal of Behavioral Science* 10, 1978, 38-45.

• Kagan, J., Kearsley, R. B., and Zelazo, P. R. *Infancy: Its Place in Human Development.* Cambridge, MA: Harvard University Press, 1978.

• Cochran, M. "A comparison of group day and family child-rearing patterns in Sweden." *Child Development* 48, 1977, 707-720.

• Moskowitz, D. S., Schwarz, J. C., and Corsini, D. A. "Initiating day care at three years of age: Effects on attachment." *Child Development* 48, 1977, 1271-1276.

• Portnoy, F. C., and Simmons, C. H. "Day care and attachment." *Child Development* 49, 1978, 239-242.

• Schwartz, P. M. "The effects of daily separations due to child care on attachment behavior of 18 month old infants." Unpublished manuscript, Feb. 1979.

• Vaughn, B. E., Gove, F. L., and Egeland, B. "The relationship between out of home care and the quality of mother-infant attachment in an economically disadvantaged population." *Child Development* 51, 1980, 1203-1214.

p. 82 *Early, largely discredited, study of negative effects of day care on attachment:* Blehar, M. C. "Anxious attachment and defensive reactions associated with day care." *Child Development* 45, 1974, 686–692.

p. 83 *Original "Strange Situation" study:* Ainsworth, M. D. S., and Wittig, B. "Attachment and exploratory behavior of one-year-olds in a strange situation." In B. Foss, ed., *Determinants of Infant Behaviour, Vol 4.* London: Methuen, 1969.

p. 84 *Temperament and attachment:* Buchanan, A. P. "The prediction of attachment behavior from the behavioral style of the child." Stanford University doctoral dissertation, 1981.

p. 86–87 *The New York Longitudinal Study of temperament:* Thomas, A., Chess, S., Birch, H. G., Hertzig, M. E., and Korn, S. *Behavioral Individuality in Early Childhood.* New York: University Press, 1971.

p. 90 *Field independence versus field dependence:* Witkin, H. A. *Psychological Differentiation.* New York: Wiley, 1962.

CHAPTER FIVE: ASSESSING DAY CARE: HOW TO INTERVIEW AND OBSERVE

p. 133 *Ten dimensions of day care atmosphere:* Prescott, E., and Jones, E. "Institutional analysis of day care." Pasadena, CA: Pacific Oaks College, 1970.

CHAPTER SIX: MAKING DAY CARE ARRANGEMENTS

p. 135 *Day care stability:* Vaughn, B. E., Gove, F. L., and Egeland, B. "The relationship between out of home care and the quality of mother child attachment in an economically disadvantaged population." *Child Development* 51, 1980, 1203–1214.

CHAPTER SEVEN: HELPING YOUR CHILD AND YOURSELF ADJUST TO DAY CARE

p. 156 *A review of technical and popular writings on the effects of maternal employment:* Etaugh, C. "Effects of non-maternal care on children: Research evidence and popular views." *American Psychologist* 35, 4, 1980, 304–319.

p. 156–157 *Classic study of the effects of a mother's attitude toward work and its influence on child-rearing:* Radke-Yarrow, M., Scott, P., deLeeuw, L., and Heinig, C. "Child-rearing in families of working and non-working mothers." *Sociometry* 25, 1962, 122–140.

p. 157 *Mother's attitude toward work and its influence on the child at separation:*

Hock, E. "Alternative approaches to childrearing and their effects on the mother-child relationship." Final Report: Office of Child Development, USDHEW, 1976.

p. 162 *Separation anxiety:* Rheingold, H. L., and Eckerman, C. O. "The infant separates himself from his mother." *Science* 168, 1970, 78–83.

p. 168 *Physiologic stress in children during separation:* Sroufe, L. A., and Waters, E. "Heartrate as a convergent measure in clinical and developmental research." *Merrill-Palmer Quarterly* 23, 1977, 3–28(b).

p. 168 *Educational Testing Service study of separation responses:* Weinraub, M., and Lewis, M. "The determinants of children's responses to separation." *Monographs of the Society for Research in Child Development,* 44, 4, No. 172, 1977.

p. 170 *Laboratory study of long versus short good-byes:* Adams, B. E., and Passman, R. H. "The effects of preparing two-year-olds for brief separations from their mothers." *Child Development* 52, 3, 1981, 1068–1070.

p. 171 *Adjustment period for one-year-olds going to day care centers:* Cohen, M. C. "The ecological validity of a laboratory measure of attachment." Stanford University doctoral dissertation, 1979.

p. 171 *Changes in attachment behavior after starting day care:* Blanchard, M., and Main, M. "Avoidance of the attachment figure and socio-emotional adjustment in day care infants." *Developmental Psychology* 15, 4, 1979, 445–446.

p. 171 *Five-month adjustment of children in family day care:* Siegel-Gorelick, B. "The influence of caregiver competence fostering and environmental complexity of children reared in day care and at home." Stanford University doctoral dissertation, 1980.

p. 173 *Mother-infant attachment in primates:* Mendoza, S. P., Coc, C. L., Smotherman, W. P., Kaplan, J., and Levine, S. "Functional consequences of attachment: A comparison of two species." In W. P. Smotherman and R. W. Bell, eds., *Maternal Influences and Early Behavior.* New York: Spectrum Press, 1979.

CHAPTER EIGHT: DAY CARE AS THE STATUS QUO

p. 180 *Time spent by parents in day care centers:* Zigler, E. F., and Gordon, E. D. "Preface." In E. F. Zigler and E. D. Gordon, eds., *Day Care—Scientific and Social Policy Issues.* Boston: Auburn House, 1982.

p. 183 *Emotional expressiveness of caregivers and children:* Siegel-Gorelick, B., Ambron, S., and Everson, M. "Direction of influence and intensity of affect in caregiver child interactions in day care and at home." Biennial meeting of Society for Research in Child Development, 1981.

p. 185 *Cyclical adjustment to day care as a function of developmental stage:* Rodriguez, D. T., and Hignett, W. F. "Infant day care: How very young children adapt." *Children Today,* Nov.–Dec. 1981, 10–12.

p. 187–188 *Questionnaire for examining caregiver burnout:* Maslach, C., and Jackson, S. E. "Maslach Burnout Inventory—Human Services Survey." Palo Alto, CA: Consulting Psychologists Press, 1981.

p. 191   *Parent-child interactions of day care and home-reared children:* Clarke-Stewart, A. K. "Observation and experiment: Complementary strategies for studying day care and social development." In S. Kilmer, ed. *Advances in Early Education and Day Care*, Greenwich, CT: JAI Press, 1979.

Additional Readings for the Interested Parent

Caplan, F. (ed.) *The Parenting Advisor.* New York: Anchor Press/Doubleday, 1978. (This is a thorough, all-around book on parenting, covering a wide variety of topics in a way that is quickly accessible.)

de Villiers, P. A., and de Villiers, J. G. *Early Language.* Cambridge, MA: Harvard University Press, 1979. (Written for the informed parent with a particular interest in language development. It is part of the "Developing Child" series. Other books in this series may be of interest, especially *Mothering* by R. Schaffer.)

Hartup, W. W. (ed.) *The Young Child: Reviews of Research.* Washington, D.C.: National Association for the Education of Young Children, 1972. (A wide-ranging, fairly comprehensive review of varying areas of child-development research, prepared by well-known researchers in their field.)

Macaulay, R. *Generally Speaking: How Children Learn Language.* Rowley, MA: Newbury House, 1980. (An easily read book on language development, which does an excellent job of gleaning from often obscure research the core of information that parents most often seek.)

Maccoby, E. E. *Social Development: Psychological Growth and the Parent-Child Relationship.* New York: Harcourt Brace Jovanovich, 1980. (A rather scholarly treatment of all aspects of research on parents and children by a leading researcher. Too technical for straight-through reading, but highly informative on each topic discussed.)

Provence, S., Naylor, A., and Patterson, J. *The Challenge of Day Care.* New Haven: Yale University Press, 1977. (An invaluable resource for day care providers. This book describes how day care can be used as a supplement for children at risk, as well as how to be sensitive to the needs of all children in day care.)

Steinfels, M. O. *Who's Minding the Children: The History and Politics of Day Care in America.* New York: Simon and Schuster, 1973. (For those interested in the day care movement as a political, social, or economic phenomenon, this is the definitive book on its history.)

Index

Dr. Bryna Siegel-Gorelick is a child psychologist at the Stanford University Medical Center and the Children's Hospital at Stanford. She lives in San Carlos, California, with her husband and four-year-old daughter.